SPIRITUAL WARFARE

MADE SIMPLE

SPIRITUAL WARFARE

MADE SIMPLE

Praying Medic

INKITY PRESS

Inkity Press LLC
137 East Elliot Road, #2292, Gilbert, AZ 85299

This book and other Inkity Press titles can be found at: PrayingMedic.com

Available from Amazon.com, and other retail outlets.

For more information visit our website at **www.inkitypress.com**
or email us at **admin@inkitypress.com** or **admin@prayingmedic.com**

ISBN-13: 978-1-947968-38-7 (Inkity Press)

Printed in the U.S.A.

To the intercessors—you know who you are,
and so does heaven.

MOST PEOPLE ACCEPT THE IDEA of spiritual warfare in principle. They believe an enemy of some sort is real. They've felt the opposition. But when the battle arrives—when the chronic anxiety won't lift, when the relationship crumbles, when a loved one lays dying—the theory of spiritual warfare doesn't translate into practice. Knowing that a war exists is not the same as knowing how to fight it. This book is an attempt to close that gap.

Spiritual Warfare Made Simple is the tenth book in *The Kingdom of God Made Simple* series. The collection began with *Divine Healing Made Simple,* which was written to demystify the principles of supernatural healing. That led to books on hearing God's voice, seeing in the spirit, emotional healing, dream interpretation, the release of power for miracles, and the exercise of authority. Each book provides practical tools that help believers overcome spiritual opposition and walk in closer relationship with God.

Book 9 in the series, *Freedom from Evil Spirits Made Simple,* focused on personal warfare—how demons operate, how they gain access to us, and how to be free from their influence. If you are dealing with personal demonic oppression or in need of deliverance, that book provides the foundation. You don't need to have read it before reading this one, but it is a natural companion.

This book broadens the focus. We begin with the basics—what the spiritual world is, who the players are, and what happened the moment you gave your life to Christ. From there we move through identity, authority, and the specific tools God has given us: the armor of God, prayer in the Spirit, intercession, discernment, dreams and visions, and more. The second half of the book addresses how warfare operates beyond the personal—in relationships, in the workplace, in neighborhoods, in cities, and over regions. We close with the disciplines that sustain a warrior over the long haul: rest, wonder, fasting, and the willingness to stand when nothing seems to change.

This book is written for anyone who wants to understand the nature of the war they have already been drafted into. A theological background or prior experience with supernatural ministry is not necessary. What you need is a willingness to take the subject seriously and a readiness to act on what you learn. If you are new to these subjects, the early chapters will give you the foundation. If you are more experienced, the later chapters will stretch you into territory most books on this subject don't cover.

A note on language: Jesus and the apostle Paul regularly used military terminology to illustrate the principles of spiritual conflict. You will find the same approach throughout these chapters. The warfare described here is not literal combat. The terms are figurative—chosen because no other vocabulary captures the stakes as precisely. Keep that in mind as you read, and resist the temptation to make the analogies carry more weight than they were designed to bear.

Now, let's get started.

~ Praying Medic

CHAPTER ONE

The Spiritual World

YOU ARE NOT A PHYSICAL body seeking spiritual experiences. You are a spirit, clothed in a body, governed by a soul. The spiritual world is not a far-off reality. It is a parallel theater of operations that intersects with the physical realm at this very moment. You are not struggling to interact with the spiritual world; you are interacting with it right now. Whether you realize it or not, your spirit is always receiving, interpreting, and transmitting signals in the spiritual domain. It never ceases doing so, and yet, many people struggle to apprehend the spiritual realm. The key is training your mind to perceive these constant interactions in the spiritual dimension.

Just as military forces use satellites, radar, sonar, and infrared to gather various forms of intelligence, you have been equipped with an array of spiritual senses. They include the ability to perceive the spiritual world through visions, to hear spirit-to-spirit communication from God, angels, and demons, and to detect the presence of spiritual beings through smell. Some encounters may feel like tingling, warmth, or a chill. There is also intuitive knowing—the ability to instantly recognize truth, discern motives, or perceive deception. These are not skills reserved for a select few; they are available to everyone.

Evil spirits—often referred to in the New Testament as demons—are a subject of some debate. My perspective, which I acknowledge is not universally accepted, is that demons are the disembodied spirits of the Nephilim: the offspring of a union between rebellious angels and human women described in Genesis 6:1–4. These hybrid beings were never meant to exist. Unlike humans, they were not created in God's image and cannot be redeemed through the blood of Christ. When their physical bodies died, their spirits remained on the earth—restless and seeking re-embodiment. They remember what it felt like to inhabit a physical body and long to interact with the material world again—but they can only do so through us. Fallen angels, by contrast, are heavenly beings who retained much of their original power and operate in the heavenly realms. Demons are earthbound, seeking human bodies they can torment and influence.

Direct Communication: Thought-Based Transmissions

Human vision requires an object to be illuminated by photons of light before it can be seen by the eye. Spiritual vision is not limited in this way. One can see an angel in a pitch-dark room. You may have a cold and be unable to smell, and yet, your spirit may detect the sulfur-like odor of a demon. Unlike human speech, which relies on the movement of air, the transmission of sound waves, and the physical structures of the ear that allow for hearing, spirit-to-spirit communication is telepathic. Angels and demons do not speak with mouths as we do. They transmit intentions and thoughts directly. One may experience this as an intuitive knowing, a thought impression, or a sentence in one's mind that feels foreign to one's own thoughts.

Many people have experienced sleep paralysis. Victims find they cannot move or speak, but merely thinking the name of Jesus or commanding the demon to leave in their mind brings instant freedom. Words are not necessary. Evil spirits respond to spiritual signals, not sound waves. Spoken words are effective only when they reflect the authority and clarity already present in your spirit. I'm not saying we should not command demons to leave with our voice. We certainly should. I'm merely pointing out that it is the state of our soul and spirit—our faith, our intention, and our identity—that matters most.

Why Demons Don't Respond to Your Words Without Faith

You may have commanded a demon to leave and found that nothing happened, even though you used the right words and invoked the name of Jesus. Demons respond to authority exercised in faith. Authority isn't a matter of what we say. It's a matter of who we are. A private in the army cannot impersonate a general and expect his orders to be followed. If the one issuing a command lacks faith or legitimate authority, their commands will be ineffective. Faith is another word for *confidence.* When your spirit broadcasts fear, unbelief, or double-mindedness, it is like transmitting on a radio without an antenna. The signal goes nowhere. But when your spirit transmits in confidence (faith) as a representative of Christ (our authority), the enemy receives the signal and obeys.

The apostle James warned that the one who doubts is like a wave of the sea, unstable in all they do. On the Andy Griffith Show, Don Knotts played a fear-filled Sheriff's deputy named Barney Fife. He had a gun and wore a badge. He was duly authorized. But when he commanded a crook to put his hands in the air, Barney trembled like a leaf in the wind. His authority was real, but no one respected him. His fear was plain for all to see. In the same way, demons can see when we operate in fear or unbelief. Despite our legitimate authority, and the issuance of a proper command, when we operate in fear, the kingdom of darkness ignores us.

In battle, clarity of communication is essential. If your spirit is conflicted—speaking one thing, while thinking another, doubting whether your words will be obeyed—the signal is garbled. Demons do not obey mixed messages. Train your thoughts to agree with your words. Align your declarations with the agenda of heaven, and refuse to transmit weak or uncertain commands. Do these things, and the kingdom of darkness will obey you.

CHAPTER TWO

What Is a Spirit?

MANY PEOPLE DO NOT RECOGNIZE the influence of demons in their lives. They may struggle with chronic illness, ongoing relationship problems, or repeated financial setbacks, but do not see these as spiritual issues. Some experience insomnia, anxiety, or persistent negative thoughts, yet never consider the possibility of a demonic cause. Actually, for most of *my* life, I did not believe demons interacted with me personally. After becoming a Christian in 2000, I learned about demons, but they remained purely theoretical. That changed on August 8, 2008, when I had a dream in which I encountered God. This experience marked a turning point for me. Since then, I have received many dreams, visions, and encounters with spiritual beings. What was once an abstract idea became a reality I could no longer ignore.

My first direct experience with a demonic attack happened late at night. I woke up, unable to move or speak, and felt as though something was restraining me. My wife, who was next to me, realized what was happening and commanded the evil spirit to leave. The demon departed. Seconds later, I could move and speak again. This experience caused me to accept the fact that spiritual warfare is not just a theological doctrine. I had encountered a demon, and it paralyzed me. From then on, I understood that I was engaged in a real spiritual conflict. A metaphysical theory became a theater of war, and I had received my battlefield commission.

The Bible teaches that God is Spirit and that we are made in His image. Our true nature is spiritual, and we must learn to use our spiritual senses, not just our physical ones, to navigate life. To understand spiritual warfare, we must know who the enemy is and where he came from.

Scripture explains that Lucifer, a high-ranking angel, became proud and rebelled against God. As a result, he was cast out of heaven along with other angels who followed him. These beings now oppose God and seek to deceive and harm people.

We do not fight alone. Angels are sent by God to carry messages, battle demons, and assist in healing. There have been times when my wife and I have sensed their presence and received clear warnings or instructions from them.

The strategies of angels are often subtle, invisible to those who are not directly involved. A friend once walked into a nightclub with two towering angels at his side. Steve was well-acquainted with his angelic escorts, but they were normally invisible to the world. That evening at the nightclub, they revealed themselves to a young woman—and the sight of them undid her. She gave her life to Christ. Heaven had claimed a soul through a demonstration that bypassed the intellect and went straight to the heart.

In any war, you must recognize your allies and adversaries. The shock of seeing an angel or confronting a demon is understandable—but it should not intimidate you. These encounters are not for fascination; they are calls to action. You must know your orders. You must exercise your authority with wisdom. You must wield your weapons without hesitation. This is the battle we have all been born into.

A person may not attribute their illness to an evil spirit, yet any disease may be demonic in origin. Someone may blame gender confusion on human causes, but the issue may, in fact, be the agenda of a fallen angel. The hosts of darkness do not want us to recognize their involvement in human affairs. They prefer we remain ignorant. When we are, we will not take up arms against them.

Whether we know it or not, whether we fight or not, the battle is raging. There is no neutral ground, no sideline where you can watch and remain safe. You can choose to train, or you can stumble through life in darkness. The battle is just as real either way. The first encounter may be unsettling, but that is when the untested will retreat, while seasoned soldiers move forward. And when the next strike comes, you will meet it not as a startled beginner, but as one who knows the battlefield and will not yield an inch.

CHAPTER THREE

Angels in Warfare

YOU ARE NOT FIGHTING THIS battle alone. This point was made briefly in the previous chapter, but it deserves its own treatment here, because most believers live and minister as though the angelic dimension of warfare is either theoretical or reserved for exceptional saints. Neither is true.

Scripture introduces angels as active participants in the conflict between the kingdom of God and the kingdom of darkness. They break people out of prisons, shut the mouths of lions, deliver intelligence under fire, hold perimeters during deliverance sessions, and show up on hillsides with horses and chariots of fire when the situation warrants it. They are agents of the King, and they take their assignments seriously.

Before looking at what angels do in warfare, it helps to be clear on what they are. Angels are not eternal beings. They were created by

God, along with everything else in the invisible realm. Paul writes in Colossians 1:16 that through Christ, "all things were created that are in heaven and on earth, visible and invisible, whether thrones or dominions or principalities or powers." The invisible, structured hierarchy of the spiritual world—on both sides of the conflict—was created and has a definite order.

Scripture describes the angelic order in governmental terms: thrones, dominions, principalities, powers. These ranks exist in God's loyal angelic host and in the enemy's counterfeit kingdom alike. On God's side, they describe the delegation of authority from the throne downward. Michael is identified as the archangel who contends on behalf of God's people.

Gabriel functions as a messenger and interpreter of visions. The cherubim and seraphim occupy specific roles near the throne itself. The most common angels—the ones sent on assignment throughout the pages of scripture—appear simply as men. Abraham's three visitors ate a meal with him. Two angels walked through the gate of Sodom and were indistinguishable from human travelers until the situation turned dangerous. The writer of Hebrews warns that some have entertained angels without ever knowing it.

The enemy's hierarchy mirrors this structure. Principalities are regional powers that shape the spiritual atmosphere of nations and cultures. The "prince of Persia" that delayed the answer to Daniel's prayer for twenty-one days was not a human official but a territorial spirit of this rank. Powers and rulers of darkness operate at lower levels, influencing institutions, communities, and individuals. Satan, once Lucifer, was the highest of the created angelic beings before his rebellion. He now operates through deception and accusation rather than authority, but the structure remains.

Understanding this order matters in warfare because different levels of conflict require different responses. A demon afflicting an individual is not the same as a principality shaping a nation, and engaging them the same way is a tactical error. It also explains why the presence of God's angels in a conflict can shift dynamics quickly—they are operating at a rank that the enemy's forces must reckon with.

What Angels Do in Warfare

The most direct account of angelic warfare in scripture is found in Daniel chapter 10. Daniel had been fasting and praying for three weeks without a response. When the angel finally arrived, he explained the delay: "the prince of the kingdom of Persia withstood me twenty-one days; and behold, Michael, one of the chief princes, came to help me." The answer to Daniel's prayer had been dispatched the moment he began praying. It was delayed not by God's reluctance but by an opposing spiritual power of high rank. It took Michael's intervention to break through.

That passage tells us several things. First, our prayers are heard immediately. Second, warfare in the heavenly realm is real and involves genuine resistance. Third, the breakthrough came through angelic reinforcement dispatched from the throne. And fourth, Daniel's part in the whole operation was simply to keep praying. He had no visibility into the conflict. He had no ability to accelerate the breakthrough. He just stayed at his post and prayed.

Beyond heavenly engagement with territorial powers, angels operate in warfare in several more ways. They guard perimeters during intense ministry. A group ministering outdoors in a region of heavy occult activity found that onlookers who gathered to disrupt the session advanced to a certain point and stopped, unable to cross an invisible line. One of the ministers saw in the spirit a ring of figures standing shoulder to shoulder around the group, facing outward. The interference never came.

Angels assist with deliverance. During a particularly difficult session, a woman's countenance suddenly changed. Her eyes went wide with awe. She described tall figures of light surrounding her, each holding what looked like a gleaming sword. She watched as chains she hadn't known were binding her were cut through. The oppression lifted. The air, she said, felt clear for the first time in years. The man leading the deliverance session hadn't seen what she saw. But the release was real, and the peace that followed changed her.

Sometimes the person being ministered to sees the angels. Sometimes demons do. A pastor working with a man who had deep occult involvement reached a point in the session where the man's chaotic movements suddenly stilled. His eyes fixed on something behind the pastor—something the pastor couldn't see. Fear filled the man. The pastor told him quietly that whatever he was seeing was there to enforce the orders of heaven. The demon departed. The man collapsed in tears—finally free.

Angels provide intelligence. The one who came to Daniel explained the conflict in the heavenly realm, told him what would happen, and prepared him for what was coming. Dreams and visions frequently involve angelic messengers delivering strategic information. The accounts in this book of receiving forewarning through dreams reflect this reality.

Angels also assist intercessors. Revelation chapter eight shows an angel standing at the heavenly altar, gathering the prayers of the saints with incense and offering them before the throne. Then fire from that altar was cast to earth. What began as human prayer ended as seismic spiritual activity, mediated through angelic ministry. Your prayers are not merely spoken into the air. They arrive somewhere. They are handled by someone. The machinery of heaven takes them seriously.

Elisha's servant woke to find the city surrounded by enemy forces and panicked. Elisha prayed that his eyes would be opened, and he saw what was already there: the hills full of horses and chariots of fire. The angelic host was in position before the servant looked. It was in position before Elisha prayed. The prayer didn't summon them. It opened the servant's eyes to a reality already present.

Most of what the angels do in the warfare you are engaged in will be invisible to you. You won't see the opposition being cleared, the perimeters being reinforced, the prayers being carried to the altar. You will occasionally see the results—the breakthrough that comes, the resistance that mysteriously dissolves, the freedom that settles in after a long battle. What sustains you in the in-between is the conviction that the hills are full, whether you can see them or not.

You are not fighting alone. You have never been fighting alone.

For a full treatment of the angelic realm — what angels are, how they operate, their roles in prayer, healing, deliverance, and territorial warfare, and how to live in alignment with heaven's army — *Ministry with Angels Made Simple* will be the next book in this series.

CHAPTER FOUR

The Soul in the Theater of War

EVERY WAR HAS ITS DOMAIN. Air combat is fought in the skies. Submarine warfare unfolds at sea. A battle's domain is chosen for its strategic value—a land chokepoint or a vital harbor. In the war between heaven and hell, the domain is neither a faraway nation nor a stretch of ocean. It is closer and infinitely more personal. It is your soul.

When God created you, He gave you a body, a spirit, and a soul. Your body connects you to the physical world. Your spirit connects you to God. Your soul is where decisions are made, and your personality resides. It's the domain of spiritual battles—where you decide whether to accept or resist the influence of darkness.

At the moment of its creation, your soul was unscarred—a pristine outpost designed to receive instructions from God and act on them in the natural world. But no sooner had it been commissioned than the war began. The kingdom of darkness leaves no post unchallenged. Like a military unit mapping artillery, it studies every vulnerability and unguarded entry point.

The kingdom of darkness wages war in the soul. Its first-order effects are on the mind. The enemy's psychological operations warp your perception, degrade your decision-making, and compromise your loyalties. Words spoken in anger, memories of betrayal, rejection, or fear looping endlessly—each a piece of enemy propaganda. Over time, repeated impressions can distort how you see yourself, others, and God. The earlier these strikes land—especially in childhood—the more deeply they set the tone for your life.

Your mind is meant to receive instruction from God. The world's systems teach us to focus on what we see and hear in the natural realm. Focusing on the physical world makes it difficult to discern when God speaks through dreams, visions, or thought impressions. But the mind can be reprogrammed to discern God's voice. It's a matter of discipline. We focus on the signal coming from the throne of heaven and block out other transmissions.

Trauma is more than emotional pain. It creates wounds in the soul that make us vulnerable to spiritual attack. Because the soul is the seat of the mind, will, and emotions, wounded parts of the soul have their own emotions, memories, and personalities. The wounded "parts" of the soul are tormented by demons that can influence our thoughts, emotions, and even affect our physical health. When the soul is compromised, it affects every part of life. When lies and wounds take up residence long enough, they become strongholds. Paul describes them in 2 Corinthians 10:4–5 as "arguments and every high thing that exalts itself against the knowledge of God." A stronghold is not simply a bad habit or a temptation. It's a destructive pattern of thought and behavior. Strongholds form with a single painful event—a moment of loss, betrayal, or disappointment.

That experience generates a negative emotion, which triggers a destructive thought. If left unchallenged, the enemy seizes on this connection, weaving a link between the event, the feeling, and the thought. Then, when something similar happens later, the same emotional and mental reaction fires automatically. Over time this cycle becomes self-sustaining. The mind no longer needs a major trauma to trigger it—just a suggestion, a memory, or the fear that it might happen again. A familiar pathway has been carved, and the enemy exploits it every time.

A stronghold is not a single lie but a cycle of repetitive thoughts and emotional reactions that the mind has learned to expect. Consider the spirit of rejection. Its starting point may be a father's absence or a friend's betrayal. The lie planted in that moment is simple: you are not wanted. Each time a relationship feels uncertain, the spirit returns and rehearses the same thought. Soon, every minor disappointment registers as abandonment. The pattern produces hypersensitivity, withdrawal, and the tendency to reject others before they can do the rejecting. Fear works the same way. A single traumatic event plants the thought that you are not safe. Later, unrelated situations trigger the same response—and even when no real danger exists, the body and mind react as though it does.

Jesus can destroy mental strongholds. He heals the painful emotions and memories, which breaks the destructive cycle. The process is simpler than most people imagine. Begin by bringing a specific traumatic event to mind—one that still carries a negative emotion when you recall it. Identify the emotion you feel. Then ask Jesus to take that emotion from you and heal the wound in your soul. Tell Him you receive His healing. Now recall the same event again. The emotion will likely be gone, but there may be a different one that is still present, repeat the process—ask Him to take the emotion and heal the wound. Keep going until the memory no longer elicits a negative emotion.

If you can't identify a specific event but are aware of a persistent negative emotion, you can start there. Simply ask Jesus to take the emotion and heal whatever wound is behind it. Repeat as needed.

For more information on this subject, see *Emotional Healing in 3 Easy Steps* and *Emotional Healing Made Simple.*

Your soul is who you are. Nothing in this book is as important as this. When your soul is healed and tuned to the frequency of heaven, nothing is impossible.

CHAPTER FIVE

The Enlistment

WHEN YOU GAVE YOUR LIFE to Jesus Christ, a change took place. You were moved from one kingdom to another, not by any outward ceremony or visible sign, but by the authority of God. Scripture puts it simply: "He has delivered us from the kingdom of darkness and transferred us into the kingdom of His dear Son." At that moment, you became part of His kingdom. You didn't apply for this war. You were enlisted into it.

The phrase "spiritual warfare" often brings to mind images of military operations—and for good reason. Scripture uses the comparison deliberately. Paul wrote to Timothy:

> *You therefore must endure hardship as a good soldier of Jesus Christ. No one engaged in warfare entangles himself with the affairs of this life, that he may please him who enlisted him as a soldier.*
> 2 TIM 2: 3-4

A United States Army soldier cannot serve until they first enlist. Through formal induction they are assigned a rank, a unit, and a mission. From that point on, their identity changes completely. They are no longer civilians. The same transformation takes place the moment you surrender your life to Jesus. You are transferred from the kingdom of darkness into the kingdom of light—not by your own effort, but by grace.

In any military organization, orders flow through a chain of command. Generals to Colonels, Colonels to Majors, and so on, until a Private executes a mission ultimately authorized at the highest levels. Authority is delegated, not self-appointed. Freelancing is not tolerated, because freelancing costs lives. The kingdom of God operates the same way. Jesus is the head, and under Him are apostles, prophets, pastors, teachers, and evangelists—given to equip believers for the work of ministry. Orders and assignments flow from the throne of God through Christ and are delegated to us. You may not always understand why you are called to intercede, deliver a word, or engage in prayer over a particular situation, but if God is your Commander, your posture is obedience.

In modern warfare, orders come through radios, encrypted messages, mission briefings, and direct commands. Some missions are long campaigns. Others are urgent and time-sensitive. Soldiers must remain alert for updates. God communicates His directives through scripture, prayer, dreams, visions, prophetic words, and the inner prompting of the Holy Spirit. Jesus said His sheep hear His voice and follow Him. Sometimes your mission will be specific—pray for a friend, confront a lie, cast out a demon, speak truth into a situation. You may never see the full scope of what your obedience accomplished, but it can move more in the spirit than you realize.

No soldier is sent to the front lines without equipment. They are issued armor, weapons, and communication gear, and trained for months on how to use each one. They drill repeatedly to build discipline, endurance, and resilience. You have been given spiritual weapons and the armor of God—but without training, those tools remain ineffective. The gifts of the Spirit and the authority of Christ must be learned, practiced, and refined. Churches, mentors, and teachers serve as drill instructors who prepare you for real conflict. Just as a soldier keeps their weapon clean and ready, you must maintain your spiritual disciplines—prayer, worship, fasting, the Word—because a rusty soldier is a liability in any battle.

Soldiers do not train indefinitely. Eventually they are deployed, with real stakes. Missions vary—rescue, reconnaissance, peacekeeping, direct engagement—but every soldier's role matters. Believers are not meant to remain seated in pews forever. Training leads to deployment. Some are called to hidden intercession, others to public ministry, healing, or prophetic declaration. But all serve in the same war. In the spiritual realm, there is no neutral ground. You are always either advancing the kingdom or retreating from it.

God is not looking for spectators. He is looking for people who understand His kingdom, obey His voice, and wield His authority. You have been enlisted, armed, trained, and deployed. The next battle may already be underway.

If you are new to this—if you gave your life to Christ recently, or if the reality of spiritual warfare is only now becoming clear to you—you are not behind. Every soldier starts as a recruit. The chapters ahead are your training. Begin where you are, move at the pace the Spirit sets, and trust that the Commander who enlisted you knows exactly what He is doing.

CHAPTER SIX

Identity

Before God gives us an assignment, we must understand our identity as a representative of His kingdom. In the spiritual realm, identity is foundational. God has established your identity in eternity. Your calling, destiny, and assignments are determined by your identity. Thus, the enemy seeks to distort your identity by imprinting a false one on you. The goal is to make you into someone other than who God intended you to be. When you operate from a false identity, you can't fulfill an assignment, let alone attain your destiny. When a believer understands their identity as a child of God, they can carry out the assignments He intended for them. (Divine assignments are discussed in a later chapter. Your divine destiny will be the subject of a future book.)

Jesus demonstrated how identity and authority work together. As He healed the sick and cast out demons, some people welcomed Him, while others rejected Him and plotted His death. His miracles were not just displays of power; they were evidence that the kingdom of God had arrived. Each miracle challenged the religious system of the day. The Scribes and Pharisees saw their influence fading because their identities were built on the idea that they needed to maintain control. When Jesus revealed Himself as the Messiah, He exposed the false identities they had created for themselves.

How often do you read the Gospels and say, "I see myself in Jesus"? Most believers shrink at the thought, worried that it might sound presumptuous or heretical. Yet Paul wrote, "Imitate me, just as I also imitate Christ." God's goal is to transform so that we reflect Jesus. Not in deity, but in function: a child of God who reveals the Father to the world. You are the only representative of Christ that some people will ever meet. If you don't allow yourself to identify with Him, you will never step fully into the life He has prepared for you. You were not only saved from the curse of sin; you were saved into sonship. You bear His image. And the Spirit is shaping you to match it. Many Christians resist the call to bear the image of Christ because they fear it will lead to pride. Seeking humility, they prefer to see themselves as unworthy of this calling. True humility is not thinking less of yourself—it's agreeing with God about who you are. If you believe you are unworthy, powerless, or barely tolerated by God, you will live from that belief. But when you believe you are beloved, a co-heir with Christ, a dwelling place of the Holy Spirit, your life will look like His. The works of the kingdom are the fruit of authority, and authority flows from identity.

Jesus began His ministry with a single, loaded word: Repent. The Greek word is *metanoia,* meaning a change of mind. Repentance is not remorse toward sin. God wants to rewire your inner reality so that your thoughts match the truth of His kingdom. In the old covenant, people expressed remorse for their sin to earn God's approval. In the new covenant, we reject sin because we already have His approval. Our thinking and behavior change because God's kingdom has come. In that kingdom, slaves become sons, orphans inherit everything, and nameless wanderers become ambassadors.

Not everyone accepts the works of the kingdom. When I started praying for the sick, I was eager to share what God was doing. My pastor supported it and allowed healing prayer in our meetings. Some of my friends had a different experience. They were asked to leave their churches. Their pastors were uncomfortable with the shift of focus and shut it down. If your identity is not secure, rejection like this can be discouraging. Jesus did not seek recognition from people. His identity was secure. He knew He was God's Son, and He lived from that truth in every situation.

Paul said we would be the fragrance of life to some and the stench of death to others. Walk in your true identity, and you will smell like freedom to some and be perceived as a threat to others. You'll be celebrated as often as you are criticized. But take heart. You're right where you're supposed to be.

On June 25, 2012, I had a dream about the importance of identity. In the dream, I was walking down a sunlit street, and every person I met was lost. They were confused, weighed down, and their eyes were dull and unfocused. As I spoke with each person, I realized they had forgotten who they were. They had no memory of their true names, and no inkling of their identities. But as I spoke their identities to them, something shifted. Their faces lit up. Their posture straightened, and their eyes came alive. They remembered. They became themselves again. When I woke, I knew the dream wasn't just for them—it was for me. God showed me that the battle I had been fighting was rooted in identity, and the way forward was not to strive harder against those who misunderstood me, but to fully embrace the identity He had given me.

When you remember your identity, everything changes. You stop chasing the approval of men. Shame no longer holds you back. Instead of shrinking back in the face of criticism, you expect God to move. You walk like a son or a daughter—a weapon in the hand of God. When the children of God remember who they are, hell trembles.

CHAPTER SEVEN

Divine Assignments

KNOWING WHO YOU ARE PRECEDES knowing what to do. Identity is who you are. Your assignment is the expression of your identity. Life in the kingdom of God is not a random sequence of events. You are not intended to drift through life hoping to stumble upon something meaningful. God has specific assignments he would like you to accomplish. The apostle Paul said we are ambassadors for Christ. The word ambassador means one who is sent. Being sent implies purpose. Your purpose is your assignment.

A divine assignment is not a task such as folding laundry. It's an invitation to participate in what God is doing. It is where your identity, your talents, your authority, and circumstances intersect with His plan in a given moment or season. Some assignments are obvious. Others are imperceptible. Some feel weighty and long-term. Others pass so quickly you'll miss them if you're not paying attention.

Many believers spend years asking God to reveal their "calling," as if there is only one thing they were born to do. They wait for something permanent, a defining purpose they can build their life around. While there are long-term assignments—lifelong callings and spheres of influence—those are only part of the picture. Assignments may be permanent or temporary. Some will define entire seasons of your life. These are commitments that require faithfulness over years—sometimes decades. But other assignments are temporary.

One of my first assignments from God was to pray for the sick and injured to be healed. Once I had mastered that discipline, God added a new assignment: emotional healing. Then came the assignment to host live streams. I wasn't excited about that one, but I grew into it. Then, I was asked to investigate and report on institutional corruption. Some of the books I've written were given to me as assignments in dreams. Other dreams prompted me to offer words of encouragement to acquaintances who were struggling with various issues. God has asked me to do things I did not feel comfortable doing. Denise and I felt there was too much risk involved in a couple of assignments. So, I politely declined. It may seem rude to say no to God, but He took it well and soon offered me other opportunities that were less risky.

You may be asked to draw closer to someone for a short time—to encourage them, to pray with them, to help carry a burden—and then, just as quickly as it began, the assignment ends. You might meet someone by chance—a conversation on a bus, a fleeting moment in a store, a brief crossing of paths—and realize afterward that heaven had orchestrated the encounter. You were sent, even if only for a few minutes. You may take a job that looks like a career move on the surface, but in reality, it is a heavenly assignment. God has positioned you there not just for financial provision, but for a kingdom purpose. You'll influence people, change policy, and reclaim ground the enemy holds.

You may be given an assignment to create, to write, to build, or to start something that did not exist before. And when that work is finished, the assignment will be complete. If you don't understand that some assignments are short-lived, you may cling too tightly to ones that have ended. The other mistake is walking away too soon from those that require endurance.

God does not sovereignly make your assignment happen without effort on your part. I occasionally receive emails from people who have waited years for God to make their healing ministry happen. When I ask these individuals whether they pray for strangers when the opportunity arises, the answer is no. They envision something grander—a more visible ministry happening spontaneously. God may commission you through a dream or a prophetic word for a specific assignment, but it is *your* responsibility to make the assignment a reality, and the way that it manifests may not match your preconception.

Spiritual soldiers must learn to recognize assignments moment to moment. Equally important is the ability to discern when an issue is not assigned to you. The enemy will attempt to pull you into battles you are not meant to fight and distract you with conflicts that drain your energy but produce no fruit. Not every problem is yours to solve. You do not have to accept every invitation to a fight. God authorizes us for specific battles based on His knowledge of us, the matters at hand, and the players involved. When you step into an issue for which you have not been assigned by God, you step outside the covering of His authority. You also waste time and resources that could be used more effectively somewhere else. However, when you operate within the bounds of your assignment, you carry the full backing of heaven.

Assignments are not always obvious. Some come as a whisper. Detecting them requires attention to nuance, sensitivity to God's voice, and willingness to move when He says move.

There are times when an urgent matter comes to our attention that requires immediate action. Or at least, that's how it seems. But is it your assignment? I receive requests from people every day asking me to intervene in what they perceive to be a crisis. I always pray about these issues. Many times, God will confirm that the issue, though real, does not require action on my part beyond prayer.

Some relationships are assignments. There are seasons that carry assignments, but they are not your identity. I've been involved in podcasting for more than a decade, but someday that season will end. If you build your identity on an assignment instead of sonship, you will struggle when God tells you it's time to move on.

God will ask you to accept unfamiliar assignments, and many of them will stretch you. Eventually, He'll ask you to release something you love. The assignment has been completed. Mature believers persist during long-term assignments and let go when short ones end.

So, how do you recognize an assignment?

Often, it begins with a nudge—a sense that God is highlighting something or someone. It may be a burden that settles on your heart, a persistent thought, an unexpected opportunity, or a door that opens without effort. It will align with your identity, even if you feel unqualified. When God told me to pray for the sick, I didn't believe in miracles. I had to submit myself to His instruction, and I made mistakes along the way. Asking strangers if I could pray for them in public wasn't easy, but I persisted through my insecurities and got on with the work.

When you step into an assignment, there is grace. It may not be an easy path, but there's a sense that you're not alone—a feeling that you're being carried along by something larger than yourself, a realization that what you're doing matters, and that heaven is involved in ways you cannot see.

As you mature in your assignment, you'll recognize the difference between striving and resting. Between obedience and busyness. Between doing something for God and doing something with Him. And that difference changes everything. Spiritual warfare is not running about willy-nilly, looking for demons to confront. It's walking with the Spirit, responding to assignments, and trusting that your obedience—whether for a moment or a lifetime—is part of a much larger victory.

You are not here by accident. You have been called. You have been sent. And right now, there is an assignment waiting to be accepted.

CHAPTER EIGHT

Identity: Renouncing and Rebuilding

IN SPIRITUAL WARFARE, ONE OF the greatest dangers is accepting a false identity. These are labels, roles, and names that we did not choose for ourselves, but have accepted over time. Often, we take on these identities without realizing it, simply because they seemed necessary for survival or because others assigned them to us. Accepting a false identity can prevent you from walking in the authority and completing the assignments God gives you.

False identities are formed gradually, often in childhood. They can be the result of trauma, hurtful words, or the influence of family, culture, or religion. Regardless of their source, they all have the same effect: they distort our understanding of who we are. A single negative comment or experience can influence our self-perception. Beliefs about our identity are reinforced by circumstances, repeated by others, and eventually accepted as truth. Most people identify themselves by these labels and respond to them as if they define them. God does not define us by our failures or by the labels others have given us. He defines us by our potential. Though Gideon was filled with fear, God called him a mighty warrior. He called Peter a rock, not a failed disciple. The name God gives us is different from the one we or others may use. If we accept a false identity, it affects how we live. If you believe you are powerless, your prayers will lack confidence. If you believe you are cursed, you'll expect defeat. If you believe you are a worthless sinner, you will shun spiritual authority.

The enemy targets our identity because it determines whether, and how, we exercise authority. When Jesus was baptized, the Father declared Him to be His beloved Son. Immediately afterward, Satan challenged His identity by saying, "If you are the Son of God." This was a deliberate strategy. If the enemy can undermine our identity, our ability to exercise authority is weakened.

False identities persist when we agree with them through what we say and what we believe. Our agreement reinforces false identities, but agreements can be broken by renouncing them. To renounce means to reject and disown a lie. You identify the false belief, withdraw your agreement with it, and replace it with the truth. Speaking the truth aloud helps to establish it in your mind and heart. Sometimes this process must be repeated until the truth is fully accepted. As you do this, you allow the Holy Spirit to bring healing (when trauma is involved) and replace deception with truth.

In the book of Revelation, Jesus promised to give a new name to those who overcome. We overcome the tactics of the enemy by waging wise warfare. The name Jesus gives you is not marked by sin, trauma, or shame. It reflects who you are in His eyes. It's not only a future promise; He intends for you to live according to your true identity now. When you accept and respond to the name He gives you, you'll exercise the authority and carry out the assignment He has given you.

Establishing your identity doesn't end once you have rejected a lie or commanded a demon to leave. In fact, that is just the beginning. Deliverance removes what doesn't belong, but lasting change requires ongoing agreement with what God says about you. He wants to transform you.

That requires you to regularly affirm your identity in Christ. It must become your default mode—the reflexive way you see yourself. God has already declared the truth about you. The Father has called you by name. The Son has provided your redemption. The Spirit confirms this truth within you. What heaven needs is your agreement—not a passive nod, but an active daily choice to align your thoughts, words, and actions with His truth. Amos asks, "Can two walk together unless they are agreed?" Agreement is necessary for change. Each time you choose to think, speak, and act according to God's view of you, you reinforce your true identity.

Scripture is both your guide and your mirror. As you read, memorize the passages the Holy Spirit highlights. You are not just collecting verses. You are allowing God's Word to show you who you are. Some passages will stand out above the rest. These should be spoken aloud and meditated on until they replace old patterns of thinking.

You must also retrain your inner dialogue. Negative or critical thoughts should be consciously rejected whenever they arise. Develop a habit of asking the Holy Spirit how He sees you, especially during times of weakness or shame. Write down what you sense He is saying, and review these statements regularly until they become more real to you than past negative experiences.

As you continue this process, be careful about what influences you accept. Not every opinion or piece of advice is helpful. Comparison, criticism, or even well-intentioned advice can undermine your sense of identity if they do not align with what God says. Reject anything that does not align with His truth.

You need not do this alone. Identity is strengthened in the presence of others who recognize your true value, even when you do not. Surround yourself with people who see the work God is doing in you, and who will affirm the truth of who you are becoming. Likewise, speak encouragement to them. Denise saw me as a writer when I did not see myself that way, and she repeatedly spoke that truth over me until it finally sank in. As you continue to agree with God's truth over time, you will observe changes. Fear will lose its influence, and criticism will have less effect. Your sense of worth will become stable and less dependent on the opinions of others. The need to prove yourself will diminish, replaced by a steady confidence that comes from being established in God's love.

Jesus modeled this flawlessly.
He was never confused about His origin—*I came down from heaven.*
Never uncertain of His commission—*The Father has sent Me.*
Never mistaken about His anointing—*The Spirit of the Lord is upon Me.*
Never in doubt about His destination—*I go to prepare a place for you.*

This clarity was His armor. No temptation, no accusation, no rejection could move Him because His identity was not up for negotiation. And as John tells us, "As He is, so are we in this world." That same clarity is available to you.

You cannot strengthen your agreement with God while also repeating negative beliefs or thoughts that come from the enemy. Each time you say you will never change, repeat words of rejection, or hold onto self-hatred, you allow these negative influences to remain. Your words and thoughts are always building something. The question is whether you are building on truth or on lies.

For this reason, it helps to end each day with a deliberate realignment. Before you close your eyes, reject any false beliefs or negative words you encountered—whether from others, from the enemy, or from your own thoughts. Then reaffirm what God says about you. It can be as simple as: Father, I reject every lie I partnered with today. I agree with You now—I am clean, chosen, loved, and powerful in Christ. Renew my mind. Live through me. Let my voice be one with Yours.

Your identity is established by God and reinforced each day as you agree with Him. You are not merely surviving the war—you are becoming a living reflection of the One who has already won it. And every time you choose to agree with Him, the walls of that fortress rise higher, the gates grow stronger, and the voice of the enemy grows fainter.

CHAPTER NINE

Command and Control

SURVIVAL IN WARFARE DEPENDS ON knowing and following the chain of command. Orders flow from the top down; responsibility flows from the bottom up. You need to know whose voice you're obeying and whose authority you carry. If the wrong person calls the shots, the wrong objectives are taken. If no one takes command, the field belongs to the enemy.

Spiritual warfare operates on the same principle. However, many Christians have accepted the idea that God controls everything that happens. This belief is often repeated when tragedy occurs, or when we try to comfort someone who is suffering. It may sound reassuring to say "God is in control," but it can lead to passivity. When we confuse God's sovereignty with the idea that He micromanages every detail, we lose our sense of responsibility. The enemy benefits when we stop taking action, believing that everything is already determined by God.

God's sovereignty does not mean that He controls every action or decision. In the military, a general gives orders and provides resources, but expects his officers to carry out the mission. In a similar way, God has delegated authority to us. From the beginning, He gave us dominion over the earth. Although that authority was lost through sin, Jesus restored it through His death and resurrection. He then gave that authority back to us.

> *Behold, I give you the authority to trample on serpents and scorpions, and over all the power of the enemy, and nothing shall by any means hurt you.*
> LUKE 10:19

Authority that is not used has no effect. If a soldier spends his time maintaining his equipment but never engages in battle, he is not fulfilling his duty. The problem becomes worse when we believe that God has predetermined every event—every tragedy and every victory, every sickness and every sin. This belief, though common, leads to passivity. If we believe that everything the enemy does is ordained by God, we stop fighting. If we think our suffering is unavoidable, we stop praying. This is not the mind of a soldier. It's the attitude of someone who has given up.

God has given each of us specific areas of responsibility. The U.S. military uses the acronym AOR to refer to an area of responsibility. An AOR may include your family, community, or workplace. You are responsible for defending these spaces. If you neglect your responsibility, others will suffer. God does not defeat attackers without our involvement. He works through us as we take action.

God does not force us to obey Him. Rather, He encourages us through a relationship. The Holy Spirit guides us, highlighting scripture, giving us dreams, and speaking through wise counsel. However, He does not make our decisions for us. We are expected to respond and obey. Jesus Himself said that He only did what He saw the Father doing. He acted in obedience, not passivity.

The enemy often tries to disguise his attacks as if they are discipline from God. He may try to convince you that ongoing oppression is something you must simply accept, or that loss, estrangement, and poverty are lessons from God. Many times, these are attacks that you have the authority to fight.

Your understanding of God should do more than comfort you; it should give you the courage to take action. God's sovereignty is not meant to restrict you, but to empower you. You have been created in His image, redeemed by Jesus, filled with the Holy Spirit, and equipped with His Word. You are not powerless. You have a role to play in advancing God's purposes and protecting what He has entrusted to you.

God is sovereign, but He chooses to partner with us. His will is accomplished through those who take their place in Christ, act on His authority, and advance His kingdom.

CHAPTER TEN

Finished but Not Final

ONE OBJECTION TO THE DOCTRINE of spiritual warfare comes from believers who deeply value Christ's finished work. They ask, if Jesus already defeated the devil on the cross, why do we need to fight him today? It's a fair question. Jesus did say, "It is finished," and He did defeat the devil, death, and sin. That fact is not in question. However, there is a difference between a victory won and a victory enforced.

Scripture explains why the battle continues. Through Adam's rebellion, humanity forfeited its God-given dominion, allowing Satan to exercise authority in the earth. He offered that authority to Jesus in exchange for worship.

Then the devil, taking Him up on a high mountain, showed Him all the kingdoms of the world in a moment of time. And the devil said to Him, "All this authority I will give You, and their glory; for

this has been delivered to me, and I give it to whomever I wish."
LUKE 4:5–6

The consequence of Adam's disobedience was nullified at the cross. After Jesus died and was resurrected, He said this:

All authority has been given to Me in heaven and on earth. Go therefore and make disciples of all the nations, baptizing them in the name of the Father and of the Son and of the Holy Spirit.
MATT 28:18-19

Satan, though defeated in the legal sense, has not yet been removed from the battlefield. Like any thief, he continues to operate outside of the law, without authority.

The thief does not come except to steal, and to kill, and to destroy. I have come that they may have life, and that they may have it more abundantly.
JOHN 10:10

Satan still opposes our assignments, causes illness, and accuses us. But Jesus has given us the authority we need to overcome him. Some people wonder why God allows spiritual warfare to continue when He could remove Satan at any time. The answer is found in God's purpose for us. God does not simply want to remove evil; He wants to raise up sons and daughters to rule and reign with Him. Just as a commander trains soldiers, God uses opposition to forge in us wisdom, patience, longsuffering, and maturity. The existence of spiritual battles is not a sign that God is absent or weak. It is the process by which we are conformed to the image of Christ. Each conflict is an opportunity to learn how to think and act as children of the kingdom.

The war is not yet over, but its outcome has been decided. You do not fight for victory—you fight *from* it. The cross has already judged the enemy; the verdict is sealed. Your task is to carry out the sentence, one battle at a time, one life at a time, until the trumpet sounds and the King returns. Your Commander has won.

CHAPTER ELEVEN

The Armor of God

THE LAST CHAPTER OF THE Apostle Paul's letter to the church in Ephesus reminds believers of the reality of spiritual warfare. Throughout his letter, he explains the Gospel, the unity of the church, and our inheritance in Christ. As he concludes, he explains that there is an ongoing conflict in the spiritual realm, and the way to remain secure is to put on the armor of God.

Finally, my brethren, be strong in the Lord and in the power of His might. Put on the whole armor of God, that you may be able to stand against the wiles of the devil. For we do not wrestle against flesh and blood, but against principalities, against powers, against the rulers of the darkness of this age, against spiritual hosts of wickedness in the heavenly places. Therefore, take up the whole armor of God, that you may be able to withstand in the evil day, and having done all, to stand.

> *Stand therefore, having girded your waist with truth, having put on the breastplate of righteousness, and having shod your feet with the preparation of the gospel of peace; above all, taking the shield of faith with which you will be able to quench all the fiery darts of the wicked one. And take the helmet of salvation, and the sword of the Spirit, which is the word of God; praying always with all prayer and supplication in the Spirit, being watchful to this end with all perseverance and supplication for all the saints.*
> EPH 6:10-18

Paul instructs believers to put on the whole armor of God so they can stand against the wiles of the devil. The Greek word translated as "wiles" means cunning plans and deceptive tactics. Satan does not usually attack us directly. Instead, he uses subtlety, accusation, and deception. Indirect attacks are more difficult to defend against. Paul explains that our struggle is not with other people but with spiritual forces—principalities, powers, and rulers of darkness.

The Breastplate of Righteousness

In ancient times, soldiers wore metal breastplates to protect their vital organs. The apostle Paul uses this image to explain that our most vulnerable place is the heart or soul, if you prefer. God provides us righteousness to shield our identity from condemnation, accusation, and compromise.

Righteousness in the kingdom is not good behavior. It is a right relationship with God. There are two aspects to new covenant righteousness. First, there is the righteousness that Jesus gives us—a gift we do not earn, which makes us right before God. Second, there is the practical righteousness worked out as obedience to the Holy Spirit. The first protects us from condemnation; the second protects us from the consequences of sin, which impede the development of godly character and leave us open to attack.

The enemy's most persistent weapon is accusation. He knows that if we doubt our standing with God, we are weak. God's gift of righteousness deflects accusations.

The Gospel of Peace

Roman soldiers wore caligae—sandals with thick soles and iron studs—to provide stability and traction on difficult terrain. Paul uses this image to describe the importance of being prepared with the gospel of peace. The Greek word *hetoimasia* means readiness and firm footing. The good news of the kingdom is that we are at peace with God. This peace allows us to stand our ground and not give in to spiritual opposition.

The peace of God operates in the midst of conflict. Peace allowed Jesus to sleep during a storm, and compelled Paul and Silas to sing while in prison. Their peace was not based on circumstance, but on the unchanging reality of God's kingdom. I prayed for a man in the ambulance one day who was having chest pain. I could see that he was frightened, so I asked if I could pray for him. I asked Jesus to manifest his peace, and the man's fear instantly left. When he asked how I did it, I simply told him that Jesus is the Prince of Peace and that He was with us.

The Belt of Truth

The Roman soldier's belt held the breastplate in place and supported weapons. Without it, the rest of the armor would not function properly. Truth serves the same role in spiritual warfare. Truth in this context is not correct information or doctrine. It is Christ Himself. Jesus said, "I am the truth." To put on the belt of truth is to robe yourself in Christ—to adopt His character, His perspective, and His words. Jesus spoke directly to the disciples. Today He speaks through the Holy Spirit.

> *These things I have spoken to you while being present with you. But the Helper, the Holy Spirit, whom the Father will send in My name, He will teach you all things, and bring to your remembrance all things that I said to you.*
> JOHN 14:25-26

The world is full of opinions and reports, all claiming to represent the truth. Jesus never lies. He is our true north. When conflicting claims fill our minds, we can ask the Holy Spirit to reveal what is true and what is not. I take in a lot of information each day from many sources. Each night, I give it all to God and ask Him to show me what is true, what is false, what is chaff, and what is worth keeping. He has never failed to honor that request.

The Shield of Faith

Paul uses a shield to illustrate faith. Everything we do to advance God's kingdom requires faith. For example, we cast out demons using authority. Authority is exercised in faith. Biblical faith is not hope or optimism. It is more akin to confidence. Confidence comes through experience. The more we prophesy, the more confident we become with the gift of prophecy. The more we release power to work creative miracles, the more faith we have for the miraculous.

Faith is a shield against the enemy's accusations. When a demon whispers that God has rejected us, by faith we choose to believe He has and will use us for His purposes.

The shield of faith must be raised by a conscious choice to trust God's word instead of the thoughts or feelings that come during an attack. Each time you choose to believe what God has said and reject a lie, you raise the shield.

The Helmet of Salvation

In battle, the head is the most important area to protect. A head injury can end the fight immediately. In spiritual warfare, the mind is the primary target. The Greek word for salvation, *soterios,* includes deliverance, safety, rescue, and wholeness. Salvation is not limited to the moment you first believed—it is God's ongoing work to protect what is His. When you put on the helmet of salvation, your mind is guarded against lies, fear, and confusion. You are reminded that you belong to God, are under His protection, and nothing can separate you from Him.

Attacks on the mind arrive as thoughts that seem reasonable: God is tired of you. You've failed too many times. Things will never change.

The helmet of salvation helps you reject these thoughts. Your past is forgiven, your present is in God's hands, and your future is covered by His promises. Paul calls it the hope of salvation, because hope filters the entire battle through the certainty of the outcome: Christ has won, and you are in Him.

The Sword of the Spirit

All the other pieces of armor are for protection. The sword of the Spirit is the only offensive weapon in the list. When writing about the word of God, Paul used the Greek word *rhema* rather than *logos*. The Bible is the logos—the written word of God. Here, Paul refers to the voice of God spoken to us at a specific moment in time, for a particular situation. Our offensive weapon against the kingdom of darkness is the revelation God provides about the issues we are facing. The rhema word of God also informs us of our calling, gifting, and destiny—issues not found in the Bible. The scriptures teach us about the nature of God— who He is. His Spirit teaches us who He created us to be.

Without the armor of God, we wander defenseless through the fog of war. With it, the path to victory is made plain.

CHAPTER TWELVE

Faith, Deliverance, and Healing

THE THREE SUBJECTS IN THIS chapter—faith, deliverance, and healing—are each treated at length in other books in this series. This chapter is not intended to replace them. The information is presented here for readers who are new to these subjects or who have not yet read those books. My goal is to give you enough information on those subjects to operate proficiently on the spiritual battlefield.

Faith

What ties these three subjects together is faith. Faith is not a preliminary topic—it is the bedrock on which deliverance, healing, prophecy, and every other form of kingdom ministry stands. A believer who does not understand what faith actually is will struggle in all of them. So we start here.

Faith is perhaps the most misunderstood concept in the Christian world, and the misunderstanding has consequences. People try to manufacture a feeling they cannot sustain, then suffer disappointment when they are not healed, when a demon does not leave, or when prayers go unanswered. The problem is not a lack of faith; it's a wrong definition.

Faith is not optimism or hope. It is not trying hard to believe something you are not sure about. It is not a feeling at all. Biblical faith is confidence—the settled, internal conviction, or certainty that God will do what He has said. When the New Testament speaks of faith, it describes a person who is not divided internally, who is not broadcasting uncertainty, who acts as though what God has said is simply true.

Jesus used the mustard seed parable to illustrate this. Some have taught that He was speaking about size—that even a tiny amount of faith is enough. But Jesus never commended small faith. He consistently rebuked it. What He commended was the centurion's great faith, and the Canaanite woman's great faith. When He compared faith to a mustard seed, He was not speaking about size—He was speaking about how a mustard seed acts. It grows. A seed produces nothing until it germinates and grows into something larger. Faith that works may start small, but it must develop before it produces fruit.

This is where the distinction between generalized and specific faith matters. Most believers have a general belief that God heals people, sets the captive free, and moves in response to prayer. But when they stand in front of a specific person in a specific situation, doubt surfaces about that person, that condition, that moment. The general faith is canceled out by specific doubt, and nothing happens.

The faith that works miracles is specific. It is the conviction that God is going to act in this situation, through your prayer, right now. That kind of confidence does not come fully formed. It is developed through experience. You begin with a general belief and take action on it— praying for the sick, commanding spirits to leave, declaring God's truth over a situation. Some of those attempts produce results. As you see God move in specific cases, your general faith becomes more precise. You develop confidence for particular kinds of situations. And that confidence spreads.

Years ago, when I started praying for the sick, almost no one was healed. I was ready to quit many times. All I had was a promise from God and a handful of scripture passages I had memorized. But I kept going, and eventually the breakthrough came—first a weak trickle, then a steady stream. The faith I had in the beginning was barely a seed. What it needed was not more effort. It needed to grow.

If your faith feels weak, do not condemn yourself. Start where you are. Meditate on what the Bible says about healing, deliverance, and the authority Christ has given you. Find opportunities to act on what you believe and take them. Each time you see God move, the seed grows. Over time, generalized belief hardens into specific confidence, and specific confidence produces consistent results.

Faith is not something you manufacture. It is something you develop in partnership with God, in the field, through the ordinary practice of showing up and trusting Him with the outcome.

Deliverance

Deliverance is simply the removal of demonic influence from a person's life. It is not a specialized ministry reserved for a select few, nor is it the dramatic, complicated affair it is sometimes made out to be. It is the normal exercise of the authority Jesus gave to every believer, applied to a specific situation where a spirit has gained access and needs to be removed.

Demons are real beings, not metaphors for bad habits or negative emotions. They are limited, however. They cannot override the human will, and they must yield to a believer who exercises authority in the name of Jesus. That authority comes from who you are in Christ. This is the principle the enemy consistently targets: identity. A believer who knows they are a child of God, seated with Christ in heavenly places, carrying the full weight of heaven's commission, issues commands that demons obey. A believer who is uncertain of their standing, operating in fear or unbelief, may say all the right words and accomplish nothing. The seven sons of Sceva discovered this when they tried to cast out a demon using the name of Jesus without the relationship that gives the name its power. The demon's response was blunt: "Jesus I know, and Paul I know; but who are you?" Authority is not borrowed. It flows from identity.

Demons gain access to people through several doors: unconfessed sin, unhealed emotional wounds, trauma, fear, occult involvement, and, in some cases, generational patterns passed down through families. Once they have access, their goal is to influence thoughts, emotions, and behavior—and eventually to distort a person's sense of who they are. The longer they hold a position, the more entrenched their influence becomes.

When dealing with demonic influence in your own life, the process begins with recognition. Something persistent—a pattern of fear, a compulsion you cannot shake, an addiction, a voice that doesn't sound like your own thoughts—may suggest a spirit is at work rather than merely a habit. Once recognized, the approach is straightforward: identify the access point, close it through repentance, renunciation, or emotional healing as appropriate, and command the spirit to leave in the authority of Jesus. You do not need to shout. Simply speak with the settled confidence of someone who knows their authority is real.

When praying for others, the same principles apply. Ask the Holy Spirit for discernment about what you are dealing with. Lay hands on the person if appropriate. Command the spirit by name if you know it, or by its function if you don't—a spirit of fear, a spirit of addiction, a spirit of infirmity. Issue the command clearly and in faith. If nothing shifts immediately, repeat it. Persistence is not a sign that the command lacked authority; it is often how authority is exercised in the face of resistance. When the demon leaves, the change may be perceptible—a release of tension, a shift in the person's countenance, a sense of peace settling in.

Not every problem is demonic. Discernment matters. But the willingness to consider that a spirit may be involved—and to act on that consideration when it is confirmed—is part of what it means to fight as a believer who understands the territory.

For a thorough treatment of deliverance—including the most common types of spirits, how they operate, and some detailed strategies for dealing with them—see *Freedom from Evil Spirits Made Simple,* Book 9 in this series.

Physical Healing

Divine healing is not reserved for gifted individuals. It is the inheritance of every believer, and the New Testament presents it as part of the normal life of the kingdom. Jesus healed the sick. He gave that authority to His disciples. He gave it to us.

The foundation is relationship. Everything in healing flows from knowing Jesus and being led by the Holy Spirit. You are not primarily in the business of healing—you are an ambassador of heaven, and healing is one of the ways that heaven makes itself known through you. Before you pray for anyone, invite the Holy Spirit into the encounter. Let Him lead. Ministry with the Spirit is a dance; He leads, and we follow.

When you approach someone who needs healing, start by asking a few simple questions. Find out what the condition is, how long they have had it, and how severe it is on a scale of one to ten. This is done partly to establish a relationship and partly to gather useful information and create a baseline so you can measure what happens when you pray. If you see improvement, you know you are making progress.

The most effective approach I have found is to command rather than ask. Many believers spend their prayer time begging God to heal, which implies that He might not want to—that we are somehow more compassionate than He is. That is a theological error with practical consequences. God has already said yes to healing. Our role is to enforce His will, not to persuade Him. Command the sickness, pain, or condition to leave. Command the affected body part to be healed. Speak to it the way Jesus spoke to fevers, paralysis, and storms—directly and with authority.

Do not be discouraged if nothing changes on the first attempt. Pray again. Some healings come instantly. Others require persistence. When I began praying for the sick, most of the breakthroughs came after four or five commands. The mistake most people make is quitting too soon.

If you see any change at all—any reduction in pain, any increase in mobility—you are making progress. Keep going.

Sometimes a health condition does not respond to healing prayer because a demon is involved. If commands for healing seem to produce no result, consider commanding any spirit associated with the affliction to leave. Jesus dealt with a boy who had seizures, not by healing a neurological condition but by casting out the demon that caused it. When the spirit left, the boy was healed. If healing is not coming, ask the Holy Spirit whether an evil spirit needs to be addressed first.

The best training for healing is simply to do it. Find willing people and lay hands on them. Begin with those around you—friends, family, co-workers. Over time, you will see some of them healed, and each healing builds faith for the next one. Spending time in the Bible and reading healing testimonies helps. But there is no substitute for the experience of watching God work through your own hands.

Divine Healing Made Simple, Book 1 in this series, covers the subject in full—including faith for miracles, how to deal with common obstacles, and detailed practical instruction.

The Warrior's Prayer Language

SPIRITUAL WARFARE TAKES PLACE IN a realm that cannot be seen with the physical eye. The enemy often works through circumstances, symptoms, and distractions, making it difficult to recognize the true nature of the conflict. To be effective, we need the spiritual tools that God provides. One of the most important is the gift of praying in tongues—sometimes called praying in the Spirit. This mode of prayer allows us to speak according to God's wisdom and timing, even when we do not fully understand what we are praying.

Not all prayer is led by the Spirit of God. Prayers that arise from our own fears or desires can be ineffective if we are not praying according to God's will. Spirit-led prayer, on the other hand, aligns with God's will. It is guided by what God reveals, and not by our circumstances. One mode of Spirit-led prayer is to pray as we are given divine revelation. We understand what the issue is because God shows it to us.

The other form is praying in tongues. When we pray in tongues, we move beyond the limits of our own understanding and allow God to direct our prayers. The words spoken are not chosen by our intellect, but by the Holy Spirit, who knows exactly what needs to be addressed. In this way, we agree with God's will, even when we do not know the details. If this seems like a cheat code, it is. God is rigging our prayers for the best outcome. When you begin to pray in tongues, you may notice a change in effectiveness. Obstacles that seemed difficult to overcome begin to shift. You may not always see immediate results, but you may sense that something has changed in the spiritual realm.

Because praying in tongues is so effective, there is opposition to its use. The enemy may try to create confusion or controversy about the gift, or suggest that it is unnecessary or embarrassing. However, when you pray in the Spirit, you are speaking things that the enemy cannot understand or interfere with. This is not just a defensive advantage; it is a way to take back ground that has been lost.

Praying in tongues also builds up your spirit. It helps you remain strong in situations that might otherwise overwhelm you. You are in communion with God. Your spirit is connected to His, and your will is aligned with His purposes. When you feel weak or do not know what to pray, praying in tongues can renew your strength.

Sometimes, praying in tongues leads to deep, wordless expressions that cannot be put into human language. Romans 8:22–23 describes this as groaning, both in creation and in believers who are waiting for God's promises. These are not simply emotional reactions. They are utterings prompted by the Holy Spirit. Such prayer can result in breakthrough in deliverance or mark the completion of an assignment. This kind of prayer cannot be forced; it happens as the Holy Spirit leads, and it is important to cooperate with Him when it occurs.

As you continue to pray in the Spirit, you may notice that your focus shifts. You might begin by praying for a specific person, but the Holy Spirit may lead you to pray for a larger issue or region. Sometimes, you will sense that the burden lifts quickly, indicating that the prayer assignment is finished. At other times, you may need to continue praying until you sense that the breakthrough has come.

When Paul instructs us to pray at all times, he is not referring to a schedule of set prayer times. Instead, he is encouraging us to maintain ongoing communication with God throughout our daily activities. You can pray quietly while driving, working, or even when you do not have words to express your needs. For me, prayer is simply keeping my connection with God open throughout the day.

Praying in tongues is sometimes followed by a sense of understanding about what was prayed. This interpretation is usually not a direct translation, but may come as a thought, a scripture verse, or a sense of direction. It is helpful to ask God for understanding after praying in tongues and to take time to listen. Writing down any impressions or instructions can help you recognize what God is communicating. This makes your prayers more focused and effective.

Praying in the Spirit requires a willingness to let go of control and to trust that the Holy Spirit knows more than we do. It's acting in faith when the details are lacking. Those who practice this kind of prayer move forward as God leads, trusting that He will accomplish His purposes through their obedience.

After praying in the Spirit, you may not see an outward change. However, you may sense inwardly that something has, indeed, shifted. Some victories are not visible right away, but they are real.

Receiving the Gift

Receiving the gift of tongues begins by asking and then receiving it by faith. This statement may cause confusion, because we are accustomed to having something tangible in our hands when we are given a gift. The spiritual gifts do not leave us with a tangible item. We believe we have received the gift, and we act accordingly. Luke 11:13 says that the Father delights to give the Holy Spirit to those who ask. Set aside a quiet time to pray and invite the Holy Spirit to lead you. Ask for the words you are to speak. Praise God in your native language, then yield your voice to syllables or sounds you hear in your mind that may feel unfamiliar. You do the speaking, but the Spirit inspires the flow. He doesn't override your will.

At first, you may feel awkward. Your mouth may form sounds that seem strange. That's normal. You might begin with only one or two syllables. Repeat them and let the language grow as you use it. Sometimes you will feel a rush of emotion or deep peace. Other times, you may feel nothing at all. You're not faking it or making it up. You are acting in faith, partnering with the Spirit.

Like any language, your prayer language will develop with use. Pray in tongues daily—during worship, on a walk, while driving. Sing in tongues, allowing melodies to rise spontaneously. Read a passage of scripture and then pray in tongues over it to receive further revelation. Use the gift often. Let your spirit speak what your mind cannot.

My wife, Denise, has prayed in tongues for so many years that it has become her default prayer mode. When she tries to pray in English and it feels labored—she naturally switches to tongues. This changed how we pray together. When we pray each day for our personal needs and the people and situations on our hearts, I lead our joint prayer in English. I pray according to what God has revealed to me—through visions, dreams, or what I sense about the situation. This prayer is based on information He has given me about what needs to be addressed and how. Denise prays in agreement, but not in tongues, in those moments, because the prayer is specific and targeted. She agrees with what I have already articulated.

But there are other times when I will pray in English according to what I see—and Denise will pray in tongues alongside me, led by the Spirit. In those moments, she may address aspects of the situation I cannot see. Her prayer in tongues may be picking up dimensions of the problem that my English prayer has not addressed. The two modes complement rather than compete. Targeted English prayer and Spirit-led tongues each do something the other cannot.

CHAPTER FOURTEEN

Prophetic Intercession and Interpretation

PRAYER IS COMMUNICATION WITH GOD. Intercession is praying for others. Prophetic intercession is prayer for another that is led by the Holy Spirit. It often begins with a subtle prompting from the Lord that you need to pray. It may begin while praying in tongues. Other times, your attention is drawn to a specific person, place, or situation, or you may simply feel a persistent urge to pray without knowing why. You may ignore the prompting, but if it is of God, it will usually remain until you respond. This is not your own thoughts or emotions. The Holy Spirit is giving you an assignment.

Once you respond, your prayer may become more focused or intense. You may find your usual way of praying changes. You might begin praying in your spiritual language. The Holy Spirit may direct your prayers toward a specific need, or you may be unsure of the exact issue but sense that something significant is at stake.

The burden of intercession can become physically and emotionally intense. You may experience strong emotions, tears, or physical sensations as you pray. This is not for public display but is a private matter between you and God. The intensity usually continues until you sense a moment of release—an indication that the assignment is complete. You may not always see the outcome, but you can trust that your prayers have accomplished God's purpose.

The Holy Spirit may prompt you to declare a specific Bible verse, make a prophetic statement, perform a prophetic act, or pray in a particular way. He may redirect your prayers to a related issue without giving you all the details. Your responsibility is to follow His leading, even if you do not fully understand the assignment.

I have a friend who has a gift for getting himself into tight spots. Just before Russia invaded Ukraine, he launched a new business there. He hired employees and was certain everything was fine. I told him it looked to me like Russia was on the verge of invading. He was unconvinced. "Nah, mate," he said. "No worries—it's all good." And then the war began.

He had to flee the country. But he couldn't bring himself to abandon his employees, so he smuggled them out—a decision that could have landed him in prison, or worse. Denise and I began praying for him daily, covering him, his family, and his employees in prayer. There was an urgency in praying for them that's hard to explain. They were on my mind constantly. For weeks, we didn't know where he was or whether everyone had made it out safely. Then one day, in the middle of prayer, something shifted. A wave of peace settled over me—deep, quiet, and unmistakable. I hadn't received a report or a phone call yet. I simply knew it was going to be alright. The burden had lifted.

Sure enough, my friend landed on his feet in yet another country, safe and sound, with his employees accounted for.

That moment of peace was the Holy Spirit signaling that the assignment was complete. The intercession had accomplished what it was supposed to do. I had been given a burden, carried it for weeks, and then watched it resolve—not because I prayed the right words or followed the right formula, but because I showed up every day and didn't stop until heaven said it was finished.

When you sense a prompting from the Holy Spirit, recognize that you are being given a specific assignment. Do not ignore it or assume someone else will pray. Respond as the Spirit leads—whether through words, tears, actions, or silent prayer. Continue until you sense the assignment is complete. When the peace comes, receive it. The outcome may not be visible to anyone immediately, but your obedience has made a difference. In due time, you may understand more of what was accomplished.

Interpretation and Prophetic Listening

Praying in tongues is not always a one-way transmission. When someone prays in tongues, the Spirit prays through them, and if you pause and ask, He will often reveal what was prayed. When the Spirit provides understanding about what has been prayed in tongues—whether your own or that of someone else—it is a manifestation of the gift of interpretation.

> *I wish you all spoke with tongues, but even more that you prophesied; for he who prophesies is greater than he who speaks with tongues, unless indeed he interprets, that the church may receive edification.*
> 1 COR 14:5

The gift of interpretation is a two-way exchange that turns intercession into tactical intelligence that benefits (edifies) the church.

Interpreting Your Own Tongues

Interpretation is not a literal, word-for-word translation of what was spoken in prayer. Rather, it is an understanding or revelation of the substance of what was prayed. This revelation may be specific or general. It may come as a thought impression, a prophetic phrase, a sense of direction, a mental image, or a scripture that comes to mind. Sometimes the understanding is given immediately; at other times, it may come later, after additional prayer or reflection.

The process is straightforward. Pray in tongues for several minutes. Then pause and ask the Holy Spirit, "What did I just pray?" Quiet your mind and wait for a response. You may receive a sentence, an impression to act, or a new perspective regarding a person or situation. Record whatever you sense, even if it seems like your own thoughts. Later, you may discover that what you received was encouraging, instructional, or strategic.

You can facilitate interpretation by asking specific questions. What was the purpose of this prayer? Was something released in the spirit? For whom was I interceding? Was this intended as an encouragement for someone? Is there a scripture that relates to what I prayed? These questions invite the Holy Spirit to provide further understanding.

Prophetic Listening During Warfare Prayer

Interpretation of tongues is one form of spiritual revelation. Prophetic listening is another, broader form of receiving information from God. Prophetic listening involves pausing to allow God to reveal details, provide instruction or encouragement, or disclose aspects of a spiritual conflict. While many believers are accustomed to speaking to God in prayer, fewer have developed the discipline of listening, particularly during times of spiritual warfare.

Prophetic impressions can come in many forms. You might see mental pictures—quick flashes of names, locations, dates, or symbolic imagery. You may receive an inner knowing, a sudden awareness of some fact without words. A verse from scripture may come to mind. You might notice a shift in the spiritual atmosphere, a sudden feeling of peace, urgency, grief, or tension.

The following testimony illustrates this dynamic. Years ago, I visited Sedona, Arizona, with a friend. We drove to Bell Rock, the location of a large energy portal/vortex. Based on what we had discerned through prayer, we suspected the portal had been polluted by the kingdom of darkness. My plan was to ask God to release His glory into the situation and observe what happened. Being uncertain of exactly what dark forces might be present, we decided to keep a safe distance away. We found a public parking area about a half-mile to the west and surveyed Bell Rock and the much larger Courthouse Butte that dwarfed it. We quickly and quietly spoke our decrees of freedom over the portal.

I closed my eyes to see what was happening in the spirit. As soon as I began speaking, I sensed a strong presence of God's glory being released. I saw a thick cover of dark clouds in the spirit that were pierced by a shaft of light. An opening appeared in the clouds that gave way to a small hole of blue sky overhead. I saw lightning strikes coming from the clouds and a release of gold dust into what appeared to be the portal itself. It was all very interesting to watch. The prayers and commands only took a few minutes. Note that I did several things simultaneously in this experience: I was observing with my spiritual eyes, listening, making decrees, and waiting to feel the sensation of God's glory. When you engage all your spiritual senses, you don't just change the world; you also know what was changed and how.

While you're praying in tongues, pause after a moment and ask, "Lord, is there anything You want to show me?" After issuing warfare decrees or commands, pause and ask whether anything has changed or whether a counterattack is coming. When something appears—maybe a picture, a word, a name, or a shape—ask whether it's literal or symbolic. If it is symbolic, what does it represent? Demons often appear symbolically as black shapes. Angels may appear as shafts of light or colorful spheres. A principality of darkness may appear as a dragon.

Prophetic impressions often change their appearance in real time. One day, as I prayed for a friend, I saw a dark, sinister castle in my mind. Then, I saw a large catapult, with the arm pulled back, ready to be fired. A flaming ball was launched into the castle and set it ablaze. Then, I saw black demonic beings scattering in all directions. The Holy Spirit gave me the meaning of the scene: My friend would be used to terrorize the kingdom of darkness.

Prophetic listening may require a mental adjustment. You may feel at first like you're making it up. With practice, you'll learn to discern the difference between soul and spirit, recognize when an impression is from the Lord, and know when to act immediately and when to record it for later action. Keep a prophetic journal. Write down what you see, hear, or sense, and review the entries regularly. Many times, confirmation of what was revealed will come later.

Compare what you receive with scripture and the character of God. Does the experience lead to deeper intimacy with Him and produce fruit? When you're unsure, share what you received with mature believers who may provide tips on discerning its source.

Prayer is not intended to be a one-way street. God has much to share with us if we're willing to listen.

CHAPTER FIFTEEN

Training in Discernment

NOT EVERYTHING THAT APPEARS TO be supernatural is from God. The kingdom of darkness is just as supernatural as anything from heaven. A sermon may sound inspiring, but it may not convey God's heart on the issue. Strong emotions can be mistaken for the leading of the Holy Spirit when they are not. Discernment is the ability to distinguish between what is from God and what is not. It protects our prayer life, helps us understand our calling, and keeps us from being misled.

There are three types of discernment that we must consider. The first is natural intuition. This is the gut feeling that everyone has to some degree. It is shaped by our personality, past experiences, and emotional intelligence. While intuition can be helpful in many areas of life, it is not always reliable, and many people confuse their own intuition with the voice of God. Intuition is not the same as spiritual discernment. The second type is the *gift* of discerning of spirits, which is mentioned in

1 Corinthians 12:10. This gift is given by the Holy Spirit, and it enables believers to identify the source and nature of spiritual activity. It can reveal whether you're standing before an angel or a demon in disguise. The third type is spiritual discernment that comes from walking closely with God.

> *But solid food belongs to those who are of full age, that is, those who by reason of use have their senses exercised to discern both good and evil.*
> HEB 5:14

This third type of discernment is developed over the years as we discuss life's issues with God. We develop sensitivity to His voice and understand His nature. His work in others is recognized by the words or actions that produce love, joy, peace, and other signs of His influence. Walking with God exposes us to what is good and right, giving us a plumbline for discerning everything else.

As you grow in discernment, you become more stable and less likely to be swayed by new teachings or spiritual trends. When something is not right, you may feel a sense of unrest, even if you cannot identify the exact problem. Over time, you'll be able to distinguish your own thoughts from the voice of God, and you won't require dramatic signs to know when He is leading you. True discernment does not make you suspicious of others; instead, it helps you remain spiritually sensitive.

When you receive an impression or sense something spiritually, ask yourself if it produces the fruit of the Spirit, if it is consistent with the character of God, or if it might simply be your own thoughts. It's helpful to write down your impressions, pray about them, and revisit them later. Spiritual discernment should be open to validation from others. If your discernment causes you to become isolated or prideful, you may have gone off track.

It is common to mistake suspicion for discernment, but true discernment is motivated by love, not by fear or suspicion. Some believe their discernment is always correct, but even the most seasoned prophets make errors. Spiritual discernment should never be used to criticize or correct others unless you are invited to do so and can do it with grace.

Ideally, sharing what we discern must come from a posture of humility and a willingness to submit to the Holy Spirit, rather than being driven by pride, offense, jealousy, or a desire to be seen as important.

Spiritual discernment helps us understand issues related to timing. When we receive revelation from God on an issue, we must know if it is time to take action or whether it is better to wait and pray.

Timing is the most difficult aspect of receiving, interpreting, and applying prophetic revelation. It is rare for God to provide timing indicators. I often receive dreams that portray matters that seem, at first, to require my immediate attention. However, I have learned through experience that He usually warns me months or years in advance. That said, sometimes the matter will require immediate attention. As the time for a specific issue God has revealed approaches, there will usually be signs of its approach. Confirmation from prophetic friends, visible changes in the people involved, or cultural shifts can all signal that the day is approaching.

Spiritual discernment must be developed gradually. It can't be rushed, but it can be nurtured and fine-tuned. As it matures, it becomes the foundation of a productive spiritual life.

CHAPTER SIXTEEN

Dreams and Visions

NO COMPETENT MILITARY COMMANDER SENDS troops into a conflict zone without first gathering intelligence on the terrain, the enemy's position, and the likely nature of the engagement. Reconnaissance happens before engagement. Dreams and visions function the same way in spiritual warfare. They are one of God's primary means of providing intelligence, issuing orders, revealing the enemy's schemes, and showing us the condition of our own souls before we step onto the field.

> *For God speaks again and again, though people do not recognize it. He speaks in dreams, in visions of the night, when deep sleep falls on people as they lie in their beds. He whispers in their ears and terrifies them with warnings. He makes them turn from doing wrong; he keeps them from pride. He protects them from the grave, from crossing over the river of death.*
>
> JOB 33:15-18 (NLT)

Many believers treat dreams as incidental, if they pay them any attention at all. This is a tactical error. A soldier who ignores his intelligence briefings will be consistently surprised by the enemy. When God speaks in a dream, and we don't recognize it as such, our assignments are at risk.

Reconnaissance: Seeing the Field Before You Engage

The most straightforward use of dreams in warfare is advance notice. God regularly shows His people what is coming before it arrives, so they will be prepared.

A few years ago, I released a series of books that initially sold well but were eventually removed by a major vendor due to a nationwide political controversy at the time. My social media accounts were suspended, along with my financial accounts. The attack was coordinated and serious, but I was not caught totally off guard. God had given me dreams about it in advance. I knew it was coming, prepared some potential workarounds, and was better positioned to adapt when it arrived. Although it was a difficult season, the advance warning meant the enemy's strategy accomplished far less than it was designed to.

This is what reconnaissance looks like in the spirit. You will not always understand a dream immediately after you receive it. Sometimes the meaning only becomes clear as the events it describes unfold. This is why I keep a prophetic journal. Recorded dreams provide a trail of intelligence that, over time, becomes a master blueprint.

Reading Your Current Position

Dreams also reveal where you are in your own development as a kingdom warrior. I once had three dreams on the same night that gave me an accurate assessment of my spiritual condition at that point in my life.

In the first dream, I was in a classroom taking a freshman English class—something I had clearly been putting off. This spoke to the fact that I had neglected my prayer language. I was behind in a discipline that mattered, and God was showing me plainly.

In the second dream, I was visiting an island infested with demons. The group I was with stayed safely at one end of the island, maintaining a careful distance from the demons on the other end. Those who wandered away from the group were tormented by demons. I knew in the dream there were a million demons on the island, and that we were safe if we stayed together. The dream illustrated that demons are real and that I needed to take their threat seriously.

The third dream involved a bank robbery gone badly wrong. My group had planned what we thought would be a clean operation, but the enemy had no intention of cooperating. What we assumed would be easy turned violent, and I had to fight my way out. The dream ended with a paramedic kit and a uniform waiting for me in a convenient, nearby elevator—a significant reminder that my training as a first responder was part of my spiritual equipment, and that I was more capable than I knew.

Taken together, those three dreams gave me a clear picture: I had neglected a key discipline, there is safety in numbers, and I was underestimating what I had been equipped to do. God gave me the dreams to encourage me to continue what I was doing well, and develop the skills I had been ignoring.

Warnings of Enemy Activity

Sometimes, a dream is a warning of an enemy assignment. When you dream that something is hunting you, God is signaling that the enemy has specific strategies aimed in your direction. These dreams are intelligence briefings. The right response is to pray, ask God for the meaning, and adjust your tactics accordingly.

Visions are similar to dreams but appear as scenes in the mind while we're awake. They can be still images or unfold like a video. They may come during worship, intercession, or quiet prayer. Like dreams, they carry intelligence about a situation—the spiritual condition of a person, the nature of a conflict, or confirmation that something has shifted. The principle is the same: God is providing information, and the believer's task is to receive it, interpret it, and act on what is shown.

Receiving and Using Dream Intelligence

Dreams and visions are calls to action. Interpretation converts raw data into actionable information. Once the revelation has been interpreted, we can take action. The first step is recording what you receive. A dream remembered but not written down will usually fade within hours. A journal preserves it long enough to be useful, even when the meaning doesn't arrive immediately.

The second step is to ask for the meaning. The Holy Spirit gave you the dream, and He holds the interpretation. Ask Him directly what it means, what the symbols represent, what the emotional tone is pointing toward, and whether the dream is a warning, a commission, a call to prayer, or a status report on an ongoing assignment.

The third step is to test the revelation. Compare what you receive with scripture and with the character of God. Share significant dreams with mature believers who can help you discern their source and the correct application.

God is speaking more than most people recognize. The ones who learn to receive what He sends—and act on it—carry an intelligence advantage in the conflict that the enemy cannot match. A Spirit-led believer with an active dream life is never fighting blind.

For a broader discussion of dream interpretation—including how to identify the source of a dream, understanding symbols, and applying what you receive—see *Dream Interpretation Made Simple.*

CHAPTER SEVENTEEN

Traveling in the Spirit

IN THE KINGDOM OF GOD, there is a kind of movement that is not limited by geography, time, or the physical body. It is often referred to as traveling in the spirit. In these instances, the Spirit of God moves the believer from one place to another for a specific purpose. This is not an occult experience, but a practical reality that God uses to accomplish His will. Traveling in the spirit is used to gather information, bring help, strengthen others, or receive revelation.

Scripture has much to say about supernatural transport. Consider Philip in Acts 8. After baptizing the Ethiopian eunuch in a desert place, he did not simply walk away to his next destination. The text tells us that "the Spirit of the Lord caught Philip away" and that he found himself at Azotus, miles away, continuing to preach the gospel. There was no human orchestration—only divine initiative, moving a willing servant exactly where he was needed.

Ezekiel's ministry included many experiences where he was transported by the Spirit to places of prophetic significance. He describes being lifted and carried by the Spirit into the temple, over the city, and into the valley of dry bones. He was moved to a location where he observed, listened, and participated in what God was doing, then brought back instructions for the people. The book of Revelation from chapter 4 onward consists of scenes the Apostle John witnessed while traveling in the spirit. In these cases, God moved His servants beyond the normal limits of time and place.

Traveling in the spirit isn't a novelty or a sign of spiritual status. It is done for a specific purpose. When God moves a believer to another place or into a spiritual setting, it's because there is an assignment that cannot be accomplished by ordinary means. The most important question to ask in these moments is: What is the purpose of this assignment? Without understanding the purpose, the experience can become self-focused and lose its intended effect.

Spiritual transport usually begins with God's direction. Attempts to travel in the spirit out of curiosity or by imitating occult practices can place us in danger. The enemy has counterfeit versions, such as astral projection and remote viewing, which are powered by the soul and can be exploited by demonic forces. kingdom transport is initiated by God, carries His authority, and is often accompanied by angelic assistance. Before engaging in this kind of travel, one should be certain of God's direction, have the authority to operate in that area, and be accountable to spiritual leadership.

One of the more common forms I've encountered is something I didn't initially recognize as spiritual travel at all. When I pray for someone who lives in another city or country, I sit at my desk, close my eyes, and pray. As I do, I'll often see the person appear in my mind's eye. Sometimes, I see myself extending my hands toward them. I pray as I'm led and move on. There isn't much about this that suggests anything unusual is happening—until I hear back from the person afterward and they ask if I came to visit them.

One afternoon, a friend asked me to pray for an acquaintance who had a headache. I agreed and prayed as I normally do. About 15 minutes later, my friend sent a follow-up message asking whether I had prayed. When I confirmed that I had, he told me his acquaintance had just messaged him asking who the strange man was who appeared in his room, standing over him with his arms outstretched as if in prayer. Apparently, I had traveled there in the spirit—though I wasn't aware of it until that moment.

Another time, a friend messaged me in the morning and asked if I had visited him that night. I told him I didn't think so. I did, however, have a dream that night in which I was visiting friends and gave each one an egg. He said I visited him in the middle of the night and asked about his injured shoulder. I then prayed for him, and he felt something like a bolt of lightning going through him. In the morning, the shoulder that had been injured weeks earlier was healed. Distance, it turns out, is not the obstacle we imagine it to be.

I've come to believe that many of us are already traveling in the spirit when we pray for others at a distance and simply don't know it. The experience is often less dramatic than people expect. There is no sensation of movement, or even the passage of time. You simply begin praying and find yourself—in a way that is difficult to describe—present with the one you're interceding for.

Traveling in the spirit is not learned from books or seminars. It develops through regular, quiet time with God—where you learn to recognize His voice, understand His timing, and follow His leading. It requires responsibility and carries some risk, but when it is done under the direction of Christ, it is a powerful way to accomplish His purposes.

More information on this subject is found in my book *Traveling in the Spirit Made Simple.*

CHAPTER EIGHTEEN

Rules of Engagement

EVERY BATTLE HAS RULES THAT must be followed. In the military, soldiers are taught the laws of war, which specify when, where, and how they may engage the enemy. These rules serve a purpose: they protect the mission, the soldiers, and civilians. Spiritual warfare also operates according to order, as a function of God's authority and under His direction. Many believers approach spiritual conflict without preparation or understanding of their assignment. When someone enters a battle without knowing their role or the authority they've been given, the result is confusion, fatigue, and sometimes harm. God expects us to be disciplined and attentive to His direction. Those who are effective in spiritual warfare wait for His guidance and remain within the confines of the assignment.

God initiates our assignments. It is important to confirm any objective with the Holy Spirit, even those that seem obviously good or necessary.

When God gives an assignment, He also provides the authority and resources needed to accomplish it. If we act on our own initiative, we do so without His backing. God's assignments are specific, and it is important to remain faithful to what He has asked us to do, rather than pursuing tasks He has not given us.

I had gotten into the habit of praying for the patients I transported. One day, I was assigned a patient with a terminal diagnosis. I received a report from the nurse before we loaded the patient onto our gurney. My EMT partner went into the room to meet the patient and family, but I spent a minute in the hallway praying first. I asked God what His plan was. To my horror, I saw the words "I will not heal." I asked two more times to verify that I had received the message correctly and got the same answer each time. Saddened, I went into the room.

My partner came out of the room looking frustrated. He anticipated that I would pray and the patient might be healed, but in talking with them, it turned out the patient had already accepted his death and was at peace with it. The family was also at peace. There would be no healing. The assignment, it seems, was simply to be present.

God's assignments are not always what we expect. Sometimes the most faithful thing we can do is confirm what He is asking of us before we act—and then accept the answer, even when it is not the one we wanted.

In the following chapters, I will discuss the source of spiritual authority, how to recognize the assignments God has given you, the risks of acting outside those assignments, and the importance of spiritual covering. Before we look at these topics, it is important to remember that victory comes from following God's direction.

CHAPTER NINETEEN

Jurisdictional Authority

JURISDICTION DETERMINES THE OUTCOME OF every conflict, whether it takes place in a courtroom, on a battlefield, or in the spiritual realm. Training, preparation, and determination are not enough if you engage in a conflict where you have no legal right to act. Authorization is essential. Without it, our efforts will not accomplish God's purpose. Demons understand this principle, which is why they respond to some commands and ignore others. We must understand the importance of jurisdiction as clearly as they do.

To operate effectively in spiritual matters, it is necessary to understand the limits of your authority, how it is given, how it develops, and the consequences of exceeding the boundaries God has set for you. Jurisdiction is not limited to physical territory. It refers to the area where God recognizes your right to exercise authority and where the enemy must respond. This area is defined by your assignments and responsibilities.

Your jurisdiction may be limited to your own life or it may extend to a larger area, depending on what God has entrusted to you. In God's kingdom, authority is always connected to responsibility. You cannot exercise spiritual authority over something you have not been given responsibility to steward. Scripture offers an example of this principle. In Matthew chapter 8, the Roman centurion understood jurisdiction when he said to Jesus, "For I myself am a man under authority, with soldiers under me. I tell this one, 'Go,' and he goes..." He recognized that Jesus had authority over sickness and death. This authority came from God the Father.

Jurisdiction begins with your own life. You are responsible for your thoughts, words, and actions. This is the foundation for exercising authority elsewhere. Your authority then extends to your home, where you have the right to address spiritual issues and establish peace. It also includes those for whom you have responsibility, such as family members, employees, people under your spiritual care, and perhaps your clients. When someone asks for your help or ministry, their request gives you the right to act on their behalf. God may give you assignments beyond your usual area of responsibility. When this happens, He will provide the necessary spiritual covering. These assignments should be confirmed through prayer and handled responsibly.

Some believers have experienced negative consequences for acting outside their area of authority. The enemy operates according to legal principles and will take advantage when you exceed your mandate. Signs that you have overstepped can include unexpected financial problems, resistance in areas that are usually straightforward, sudden illness that does not respond to prayer, ongoing mental fatigue, or dreams that indicate you have entered an area without authorization. When you act outside of God's assignment, you lose His protection. I had a dream years ago where I saw the Commander of the Lord's army visit Earth. He inspected His troops and became angry when He learned that people had been teaching on issues He had not authorized them to teach, which was causing confusion. Most people had no idea they needed authorization.

God usually starts by giving you responsibility over small areas. As you are faithful in these areas, He increases your authority. Authority grows as you demonstrate obedience and attention to God's instructions. As you mature and prove trustworthy, He may expand your area of influence and allow you to address greater challenges. You might receive confirmation that your level of authority has increased through a prophetic word or a dream. A few years after God had asked me to pray for my patients in the ambulance, I heard a voice in the middle of the night say, "Your level of authority is increasing."

Once you have been given authority, it is important to steward it. The enemy will try to undermine or take what has been entrusted to you. Authority is honored when we live with integrity, avoiding deception, pride, and compromise. Pray for those under your care and make sure you remain aligned with God's assignments. If you notice unrest or resistance, ask God if something has changed or if you've neglected your responsibilities. Maintaining your authority is a matter of stewarding what God has entrusted to you.

CHAPTER TWENTY

Spiritual Covering

SOLDIERS RELY ON THE SUPPORT of their unit and the guidance of their leaders when they go into battle. In the same way, spiritual warfare is not meant to be done alone. No matter how experienced or spiritually gifted we are, we need the protection that comes from proper alignment in God's kingdom. Scripture calls this spiritual covering. Covering allows us to serve effectively and safely. Without it, even those who are well prepared can become vulnerable to unnecessary risks.

Spiritual covering includes both relationships and structure. It's choosing to submit to godly authority. It provides protection from spiritual attacks, guidance when we are uncertain, prayer support in difficult times, and correction when we make mistakes. Covering does not eliminate challenges, but it reduces their impact and ensures we do not face them alone. The goal of covering is not to make us dependent, but to provide safety, equip us, and help us stay focused on what God has called us to do. Jesus demonstrated the importance of alignment with authority. Although He was fully divine, He said, "I do nothing on My own authority, but speak just as the Father taught Me." He did not act outside the Father's will. His authority came from being aligned with the Father. Every miracle, word, and action was done according to the Father's timing.

Spiritual covering can take different forms. It may come from church leaders who teach us, from mentors who offer guidance and prayer, from ministry teams that provide training and support, or from a marriage where spouses care for each other. For most people, the local church is where they experience covering. In a healthy church, believers are known, equipped, held accountable, and sent out to serve. The specific form of covering is less important than being aligned with others who know you, pray for you, speak truth to you, and support you in difficult times.

Isolation increases our vulnerability to attack. We're more likely to be deceived, discouraged, or lose focus when serving God alone. Without covering, we may not recognize our own weaknesses and engage in battles we were not meant to fight. When others commission us, we carry their support and authority. Acting on our own leaves us without that support.

Not everything that is called spiritual covering is genuine. Sometimes, what is referred to as covering is actually control. True covering helps us grow, corrects us in love, and releases us to serve at the right time. False covering tries to manipulate or restrict us through fear. If your voice is not heard, your calling is suppressed, or fear is used to enforce compliance, this is not true covering.

In God's kingdom, covering and being sent out work together. Believers are meant to serve with the support and training of those who have prepared and released them. Doing ministry, especially deliverance, without covering can lead to problems. Starting a new work for God without being sent by others is risky. I'm not suggesting it doesn't happen. But facing spiritual challenges without a support network makes one vulnerable to attack. Living under covering is wisdom, not weakness. It's accepting feedback, asking others to pray for you, and staying connected to a community of believers. It encourages you to seek guidance from the Holy Spirit and from trusted relationships. Instead of acting alone, you submit your plans for discernment and avoid potentially disastrous mistakes. Others may see things you miss, and their support reduces your exposure to risk. It's called covering because it shelters you from the storm.

Jesus did not serve alone. He listened to His Father, received guidance from the Holy Spirit, and spent time with His friends. He valued connection, alignment, and staying focused on His mission. You may have a calling and be equipped for ministry, but it is important to ask who provides you with covering. Who notices when you are struggling? Who prays for you without being asked? Who corrects you when you go off course? Who sends you when it is time to move forward? In God's kingdom, having answers to these questions can make the difference between success and unnecessary hardship.

CHAPTER TWENTY-ONE

Divide and Conquer

THE ENEMY'S STRATEGY IS TO divide us from one another by undermining relationships that keep us safe. When unity, submission, and accountability are intact, the enemy's access is limited. When they are not, a breach opens that he is quick to exploit. Spiritual warfare is relational before it is tactical. Broken trust, introduced offense, and cultivated suspicion accumulate slowly until the bond between believers is frayed. Proverbs teaches that isolation leads to poor judgment. Cut off from constructive feedback, prayer, and the collective discernment of others, you are left relying on your own emotions and discernment rather than the guidance of the Holy Spirit speaking through those around you.

A common tactic is to generate offense toward those in authority. Sometimes the offense is legitimate—leaders will always make mistakes. But a legitimate grievance that might be easily settled can be amplified out of proportion and replayed until the relationship seems beyond repair. Thoughts like "they don't recognize your potential" or "you don't need them" appeal to pride and old wounds, making distance feel like wisdom. If a leader is abusive or manipulative, leaving is the right call. But leaving an unhealthy situation is not the same as rejecting spiritual covering altogether.

The enemy may also reopen old wounds—past betrayals in church, abandonment, or childhood trauma. Unresolved pain can make it difficult to extend trust, even in a healthy environment. Everyone needs support regardless of their gifts or spiritual maturity, and believing you are safer alone is precisely what leaves you most exposed.

A subtler version of the same tactic is a manufactured sense of spiritual superiority—the quiet conviction that you are the only one who truly sees, or that you have outgrown your leaders. This is not growth; it is isolation masquerading as promotion. David was anointed king while Saul still sat on the throne, yet he remained submitted to authority until God Himself changed the situation. God's anointing operates within spiritual covering, not in its absence. Isolation creates compounding vulnerabilities. Without others, there is no one to offer an objective perspective and no support group when you are unjustly accused. Jesus sent His disciples out in pairs and built His Church as a unified body because connection to others is a form of protection.

When covering breaks down through failure or broken relationships, the pain can make you question whether the concept is even worth pursuing. It is. God's design for spiritual covering does not change because a particular expression of it failed. The answer is to rebuild it, and it need not be in a formal church setting. You may find fellowship in a house church, a circle of friends, or a mentor who prays for you without being asked. I do not attend a weekly church service. My fellowship is mostly online, and I have a trusted group of mature believers who offer advice and support. Importantly, these people have carte blanche permission to speak to any area of my life, especially when God highlights a particular issue to them.

Restoring covering after it has been broken requires courage and humility in equal measure. Begin by acknowledging any hardness or self-reliance that developed during the isolation—even when separation was necessary. Unresolved bitterness and independence create openings for the enemy. Then ask God to bring the right people, and when He does, engage with them fully. Allow yourself to be known, corrected, and encouraged, not merely observed from a distance.

You were never meant to fight alone. Find your tribe. Honor your covering. Guard the unity you build as though lives depend on it— because in the spiritual realm, they do.

CHAPTER TWENTY-TWO

Partnering with Difficult People

A RECONNAISSANCE UNIT HAS LOCATED a key bridge that the enemy is using. The bridge must be destroyed, but the demolition team is led by someone the recon group despises. Old conflict, personality clash, a history of friction—the reasons don't matter. What matters is that without the demolition team, the mission fails. The bridge stays up. The enemy keeps using it. Personal feelings have become a tactical liability.

This scenario plays out in spiritual warfare more often than most of us would like to admit.

God rarely assembles a team of people who are naturally compatible. The body of Christ is made up of gifted individuals with different temperaments, varied backgrounds, and odd ways of perceiving the world. Prophetic people in particular can be difficult to work with. They often see things others don't, communicate in ways that don't follow the expected script, and operate from an intensity that can feel abrasive. Their idiosyncrasies are sometimes inseparable from their gifting—the same sensitivity that allows them to receive from God can make them hard to read and harder to manage. That does not make them less valuable. Consider the possibility that they may be more necessary and more costly to dismiss.

Christians are also, if we are honest, prone to trust issues. Effective spiritual community requires vulnerability, and vulnerability is often exploited. Some believers have been burned badly enough that their guard is permanently up. They need evidence before they extend trust to anyone. They want credentials verified before they follow anyone's lead. That caution is understandable. But it can become a weapon the enemy uses to keep gifted people from working together. If you require full confidence in someone before you will partner with them, you will spend a great deal of time alone watching the enemy cross the bridge.

There will be seasons when God asks you to serve under someone whose style grates on you. Their approach may seem imprecise, their manner offensive, their methods unbiblical. You may be temporarily assigned to assist in an operation you didn't design, led by someone you would never have selected. The question is not whether your assessment of them is accurate. You may be right about their flaws. The question is whether God's plan outranks your need for evidence of someone's qualifications.

It usually does.

Gideon was a poor choice by any military standard—hiding in a winepress when God found him, the youngest in the weakest clan. The whole arrangement seemed sketchy. David was the son nobody thought to bring in from the field when the prophet came to anoint a king. The disciples were uneducated fishermen who lacked religious training. God wasn't concerned about their lack of credentials.

The enemy understands something about this that many believers do not: a fragmented team accomplishes nothing. Division does not have to be dramatic to be effective. A low-grade irritation, a preference for working alone, a habit of mentally disqualifying people whose gifts look different from yours—these are enough. The mission stalls. The bridge stays up. And no single person can be blamed because no single act of rebellion occurred. It simply died of friction.

Spiritual warfare is almost always a group effort. Some of the most gifted warriors in the kingdom are also the most difficult to work with. That is not a coincidence. The enemy targets the relational friction around high-capacity people because neutralizing the relationships neutralizes the gifting. If he can keep the recon unit and the demolition team from working together, he doesn't need to defend the bridge.

Setting aside a grievance for the sake of a mission is not weakness or compromise. It's admitting that the kingdom matters more than being right. It's not blindly trusting someone, pretending a conflict doesn't exist, or endorsing everything about how they operate. It's subordinating your preferences to the assignment. You do your part. You let them do theirs, trusting that God, who issued the orders, knows who He's putting in the field. It's the practical outworking of faith.

Advancing the kingdom must be the highest priority. That priority will cost you something. Sometimes, it's comfort or the satisfaction of working only with people you have fully vetted. It may cost you the right to be understood. Pay the price. The mission is worth more than the grievance, and God will sort out the rest after the bridge comes down.

Discerning Your Areas of Authority

AUTHORITY IS NOT AN ABSTRACT concept. It is given for specific purposes, in specific places, and over particular areas of influence. God assigns it to His people for particular situations and expects us to know where we are currently assigned. Many believers misunderstand this and attempt to engage in spiritual warfare in areas where they have not been given authority, while neglecting the responsibilities God has actually given them. To be effective, we need to identify the areas where we have been given authority, understand how that authority works, and avoid becoming involved in battles to which we have not been assigned.

Authority comes from Jesus, who said, "All authority in heaven and on earth has been given to Me. Therefore, go." He delegates authority to us for specific assignments. When we act outside of the authority He has granted, we put ourselves at risk. The most effective spiritual warfare happens in the areas where God has assigned you. Authority is connected to stewardship, and it starts with the places where God has placed you. Your home, neighborhood, workplace, or school are often the first areas you are responsible for.

Authority is also given through relationships. If you are responsible for a family, a team, or a ministry, those under your care are within your sphere of authority. Authority is not permission to control everyone. It's a responsibility to pray for them, protect them, and look after their spiritual well-being. Parents have authority over their children, pastors over their congregations, and mentors over their disciples. When someone chooses to come under your care, you have a measure of authority from God to act on their behalf. You also have a responsibility to exercise authority in ways that benefit them.

At times, God may give you a strong sense of responsibility for a city, a nation, or a particular cause. If this burden is confirmed through prayer, prophetic revelation, and open doors, it may indicate a new assignment. However, not every burden that you sense requires action. Some are meant only for prayer. When a person, place, or issue comes to your attention, ask God whether you are meant to engage directly or simply pray about it.

A sign that you've been given an area of responsibility is when you see both positive results and opposition. The place where you face the most spiritual conflict is often the place where you have the most authority. If you notice repeated attacks in a certain aspect of your life, consider whether God has assigned you to exercise authority there. When I first began operating in healing and miracles, demons took note of my activities and attacked me regularly. In time, I learned how to exercise authority over them, and the attacks diminished. Ongoing conflict, continual success, and increased influence indicate that you have found your assignment.

Problems arise when we try to take on responsibilities that God has not given us. It is easy to be drawn into issues that seem urgent, such as national politics or territorial battles, but if God has not assigned you to these areas, you do not have the authority to act. The result is often exhaustion, lack of results, problems at home, and sudden sickness. Authority is developed by being faithful in the areas God has assigned to you.

When you operate within the sphere God has assigned, your actions are marked by clarity and peace, even in the face of resistance. You will notice changes resulting from your prayers and actions, and you will sense the support of the Holy Spirit.

God does not normally give us a large sphere of responsibility at first. He starts by giving us a small area to look after. As we remain humble, submit to spiritual oversight, and faithfully steward what He has given us, He increases our responsibility. Authority grows through faithfulness. As Jesus said in the parable of the talents, "You have been faithful with a few things; I will put you in charge of many things."

If you are unsure what your current assignments are, ask God to show you. Ask Him where you are meant to serve, who you should partner with, and what areas you should focus on. Ask whether you've taken on responsibilities that aren't yours, or whether you're seeking new assignments before finishing the ones He has already given you. God will answer and equip you for what He has called you to do. Authority is exercised in faith. Another word for faith is confidence. When you are confident in your assignment, the kingdom of darkness doesn't stand a chance.

CHAPTER TWENTY-FOUR

Warfare in the Marketplace

PETER WAS A FISHERMAN—NOT A rabbi, or a priest. Not a man of high religious standing. He worked in a boat, caught fish, and smelled like it. When he first encountered Jesus, he was cleaning and mending nets after a fruitless night on the water. Jesus climbed into Peter's boat and used it as a platform. When the teaching was done, He told Peter to row out and let down the nets again.

Peter's reply was the answer of an exhausted professional who had just had a bad night: we've been at this all evening and caught nothing, but if you say so, I'll try. The catch that followed was so large it began to sink the boat. God blessed Peter's business the moment he allowed his workplace to be used for the kingdom.

That exchange has something to say to every believer who spends most of their waking hours in a workplace that has nothing to do with church.

Your job is not a secular interruption to your ministry. For most people, the workplace is the primary mission field in which God has placed them—a sphere of influence, an area of responsibility, and a theater of operations that no pastor or traveling minister will ever reach. The enemy understands this, which is why he spends so much effort convincing believers that the two worlds must stay separate.

The separation is a lie.

Fear as the Primary Weapon

The most common form of spiritual warfare in the marketplace is not a direct demonic attack. It's a manufactured fear—the creeping anxiety that if you allow God into your professional life, something bad will happen. You'll lose your job. Your colleagues will think you're strange. Your manager will call you in. Your career will end.

When God challenged me to pray for my patients, I had anxiety over it. Silently praying in the back of the ambulance didn't take much faith. Asking a stranger if they wanted me to pray with them in the middle of a crowded Emergency Department terrified me. Someone would notice, complain to a manager, and get me in trouble. The other fear was being rejected, which turned out to be groundless. In over a thousand public prayers—roughly half on the job, half in public places—I can remember only two or three people who declined. The Pacific Northwest has the lowest church attendance in the country. I expected people would tell me to buzz off, but I found the opposite. People who had no faith, no church background, and nothing but skepticism toward religion were deeply moved when a stranger thought to ask.

The fear the enemy manufactures is disproportionate to the actual risk. That disproportion is the tell. Any time you find yourself paralyzed by a fear that doesn't match the reality of the situation, it's worth asking whether you're operating on accurate intelligence or on the enemy's propaganda.

I did eventually get called into my manager's office. An Emergency Department nurse filed a complaint after seeing me pray with a patient in the hospital. My manager asked about it. I explained that I always ask permission before praying and always respect a refusal. He was reasonable. His only concern was avoiding behavior that generated customer complaints. He told me I could continue, with two conditions: always ask first, and keep it to the ambulance whenever possible. That was it. The confrontation I had dreaded for months lasted 10 minutes and cost me nothing.

I had a dream around that time that clarified the spiritual reality behind the situation. In the dream, I was on the run from an enemy and took refuge in a hospital. I put on scrubs and blended in with the staff. When an agent of the enemy showed up, I'd pull a surgical mask over my face and duck down a hallway. As long as I didn't draw attention to myself, they never found me. The dream was God's way of telling me I was protected in the environment where I worked. I could operate freely as long as I stayed within the bounds of the assignment and didn't go looking for unnecessary confrontation. Anonymity, in that season, was a tactical asset. Not every piece of ground needs to be taken loudly.

Your Workplace is Your Assignment

Most believers think of their AOR in terms of family and neighborhood. But the workplace deserves the same attention. You spend more waking hours there than almost anywhere else. You have sustained relationships with the people there—relationships deep enough to actually minister to them, which is something no stranger on the street has. The degree to which you'll be effective in ministry with anyone is proportional to the trust you've built with them.

I had a slow shift one day with a partner I didn't know well. We talked for hours—dreams, healing, the things God had done. That afternoon, she mentioned an old car accident that had left her with chronic pain between her shoulder blades. By the time I asked if she wanted to be healed, the relationship was already established. She was comfortable. She said yes. I put my hand on her back and commanded the pain to leave. It did. That healing would not have happened in the first five minutes of the shift. It happened because a slow day allowed time to build a relationship, and the relationship created the opening. That's how the kingdom usually advances in a workplace—through the slow accumulation of trust, followed by a moment when someone's need and your willingness intersect.

There are things worth keeping in mind as you operate in the workplace. Your employer hired you to work, and they have a legitimate right to expect productivity. Being a poor employee in the name of ministry is not a kingdom strategy; it's a liability. Treat your employer's time with respect. Treat customers and colleagues well. Be excellent at what you do. Proverbs 16:7 says that when a person's ways please the Lord, He makes even their enemies to be at peace with them. Excellence and integrity are forms of spiritual authority. They open doors that aggressive evangelism can't.

The Risk and the Return

There are risks in allowing God to operate through you in a professional context. You'll occasionally be met with skepticism. You may face a complaint. In some parts of the world, overt expressions of faith in the workplace carry more serious costs—harassment, termination, legal exposure. These risks are real and shouldn't be minimized.

But Peter's nets were overflowing before he reached the shore.

God doesn't just impact the lives of individuals in the workplace. He blesses the work itself when it is offered to Him. When Jesus taught from Peter's boat, it led to the largest catch of Peter's career. The material blessing was proportional to the risk he took when he rowed back out. I'm not suggesting you'll become a millionaire, but God can increase your productivity when you allow His kingdom a place in your work environment.

The fear of discipline that the enemy uses to suppress marketplace ministry isn't without basis, but it has been inflated far beyond its actual size. In the United States, the Constitution protects your right to pray with willing people. Courts have consistently upheld that right. The American Center for Law and Justice (ACLJ) and similar organizations exist specifically to defend believers who face retaliation for exercising their rights. Institutional resistance is real but far more manageable than the enemy wants you to believe.

And on the other side of that resistance: a partner healed in the ambulance, an intubated woman reaching for your hands in a hospital elevator in front of four witnesses because she needed to pray, and you were the only one she knew to ask, colleagues who come to you week after week because something happened the first time and they want more of it. The return on the risk is real, personal, and the kind of fruit that grows only in the mission field you're standing in right now.

You were not placed at your job by accident. You are a kingdom ambassador no matter where you are.

CHAPTER TWENTY-FIVE

Spirit-Led Mapping

GOD GIVES EACH OF US a specific area of responsibility. These assignments are not given by chance. They are often tied to your calling, your life experiences, the wounds God has healed, or the battles you've already fought. If you want to know your AOR, ask yourself: What burden has God placed on my heart repeatedly? What injustice do I notice that others overlook? Where do I see spiritual patterns that others miss? When you can answer these questions, you are likely close to discovering an assignment.

The U.S. military gathers intelligence on specific geographic regions. An intelligence operator who works in the Central Command area of responsibility concerns himself with the terrain, population centers, terror threats, strategic assets, and political conditions in the Middle East. Intelligence operatives analyze information within their AOR and report to their superiors. There is a spiritual analog to this dynamic.

Spiritual mapping is listening to the Holy Spirit to discern the spiritual condition of a place or situation. Think of it like a reconnaissance team surveying the land before a battle. In spiritual mapping, you identify strongholds, lies, patterns of sin, and enemy activity in a region or community. This might include the presence of territorial spirits, witchcraft, cult activity, generational sin, past bloodshed, injustice, agreements with darkness, or large-scale trauma. The goal is to understand the spiritual landscape so you can pray with insight, use your authority wisely, and accomplish the objectives God has in mind. The Apostle Paul explained that we can know God's thoughts.

> *"For who has known the mind of the Lord that he may instruct Him? But we have the mind of Christ."*
> 1 COR 2:16

Begin by listening to the Holy Spirit in prayer. Ask God what He wants you to notice about the place or situation. He may reveal religious systems of control, injustice, past bloodshed, witchcraft, or agreements with idols. You may sense grief in the atmosphere or feel that God wants to bring revival. As you listen, God may give you visions, words, dreams, or physical sensations. Pay attention to patterns or repeated impressions. Your job is to gather information, pray about its meaning, and share it with trusted intercessors.

As you examine the spiritual atmosphere, you may notice cycles of addiction, suicide, violence, racism, bloodshed, or generational poverty. These patterns often point to unrepentant sin or long-standing agreements that need to be broken. Do not make assumptions or assign blame. Your role is not to accuse, but to be the vessel God uses to address the issue. Ask God how He wants you to respond to what He reveals. This may include repenting on behalf of others, releasing forgiveness, declaring God's truth against lies, praying over specific locations, worship, taking communion, or anointing with oil. You may be led to organize a prayer walk or pray specific prayers. Sometimes God will ask you to bring His peace into a place dominated by fear. Let the Holy Spirit guide your actions.

I lived for 16 years just outside of Olympia, Washington. The city has long been a haven for witchcraft and the occult. Friends have observed that the locations of houses where witchcraft is practiced form specific geographic shapes on a map. Olympia is home to many forms of darkness, but God has shown me, through visions, dreams, and visitations, that He plans to bring revival there. When I first became interested in healing, I joined a group of Christian friends who set up a tent at various new age fairs hosted by the city. Our tent was often pitched near those of fortune tellers and shamans who sold their services for cash or credit. Our group brought prophetic words, emotional healing, miracles, and delivered God's love—at no charge. In that season, Olympia was my AOR. My fellow soldiers and I took the fight to the kingdom of darkness. My personal calling was not to wage warfare against the demonic system directly. It was the same calling Peter, James, and John had been given—to heal the sick and proclaim the kingdom. Yours may be different. My assignment in Olympia was temporary. I've since relocated, but others are still there faithfully doing the work. One day, Olympia will experience the revival God highlighted to me.

The purpose of spiritual mapping is not just to collect information, but to see lasting change. When you understand the spiritual landscape, you can respond with love, truth, authority, and peace. You will know where to act, where to pray for life, and where to break agreement with things that bring harm. Seeing what God sees helps you know how to respond.

Ley Lines

Sometimes, spiritual mapping reveals a network of influence that stretches across an entire region, not just a single location. Some people refer to these as occult ley lines—territorial grids that are maintained by historic covenants, bloodshed, or ongoing idolatry.

Occult practitioners try to use God's creation by exploiting convergence points or centers of power to build networks of spiritual control. These networks can show up as regional strongholds of idolatry, slavery, sexual sin, or other ungodly practices. They rarely exist alone. Together, they form a grid of influence, connected by ritual, agreement, bloodshed, or injustice. The goal of all this is to secure spiritual territory and resist the advance of God's kingdom.

Some battles require us to confront powers that are deeply embedded in an infrastructure of darkness. What we are dealing with here is not merely oppression on an individual level, but a territorial power supported by legal access points, demonic alliances, and old covenants. That is why some cities remain trapped in cycles of poverty, lawlessness, or idol worship.

Most territorial grids are hidden in plain sight—behind historic landmarks, inside respected institutions, empowered by longstanding policies, or concealed in forgotten covenants. Sometimes, physical objects like obelisks or altars serve as focal points, but the real power is not in the object. It is in the agreement. Satanists are often compelled to tell the truth about what they are doing because they believe in the law of karmic retribution if they lie, and what they intend to do requires your agreement. Whenever people make a covenant with darkness, knowingly or not, they give permission for spiritual forces to occupy and exert influence. This can happen in families, cities, or entire regions. Until those agreements are broken, the grid remains.

Before you try to dismantle a demonic system, you must first discern what you are dealing with. This requires humility and a willingness to listen. Ask the Holy Spirit to reveal any hidden structures. Those who pray or do spiritual mapping often notice patterns—repeating geographic markers, specific sins tied to locations, or spiritual power that grows stronger near certain landmarks. What kinds of sin or suffering have persisted in this place over time? Are there cycles that seem to be reinforced by the land itself? Do past events, treaties, or rituals give the enemy legal ground? Ask God to reveal the spiritual grid so you can carry out His plan of redemption.

Once you have discerned the lay of the land and identified traps to avoid, you can begin intercession. Warfare against the enemy's grid involves stepping into your role as a son or daughter of the King and operating within your assigned authority. The Holy Spirit may lead you to repent on behalf of others, renounce covenants made with darkness by a bloodline, a government, or a region, or prophesy over the land, reminding it that it belongs to God. He may instruct you to pray at specific locations, take communion, anoint the land with oil, or worship in places that were once defiled. Navy SEALs are most effective when no one knows they are present. The same is true here. Perhaps one of the most powerful tools in dismantling territorial networks is worship—not the performance of songs, but the true exaltation of Jesus, where His name has been dishonored. Worship not only reclaims ground; it reestablishes dominion. When you release authentic praise in a contested area, you are placing a flag of heaven in enemy territory, declaring that the King is present and that the dominion of darkness is over.

Finally, warfare on this scale should never be undertaken alone. There is safety in spiritual community, pastoral covering, and mutual accountability. Do not engage every territorial spirit you become aware of. Confirm your assignment. Before any engagement, ask whether this is a battle God has commissioned you to fight, or simply one He wants you to witness in prayer. The goal is not to stir up war. It is to establish peace—the kind that flows from the triumph of Christ and pushes out every rival claim to His throne.

CHAPTER TWENTY-SIX

Mental Preparedness

THE BATTLE FREQUENTLY BEGINS IN the mind, long before a soldier enters the battlefield. Military training recognizes that the mind determines how far the body can go. If the mind is prepared to endure difficulty, the body will follow. But if the mind is weak, a strong body will fail under stress.

The mind is the primary domain where spiritual battles are fought. If the enemy can influence your thoughts, he can affect your emotions, undermine your determination, and negate your actions before the conflict begins. Your mind is strategic terrain. From it, you see the battlefield, choose your targets, and direct your resources. A mind fortified by truth is nearly impossible to overrun. Lies bounce off its walls. Fear finds no foothold. But a mind left undefended becomes a staging ground for the enemy's operations—a place where accusations, doubts, and temptations are launched against the heart and spirit.

Your mind must be prepared before you face challenges. As believers, we need to train our minds to respond with truth when difficulties arise. Meditating on scripture and the revelation we receive from God is not just a religious habit; it is intentional programming that equips us to act when the time comes.

In the early years of my healing ministry, I struggled with fear of what people might think of a random stranger praying in public. I often doubted that the person I prayed with would be healed. I needed to deal with fear and doubt, so I reminded myself of the many dreams God had given me in which I prayed for people in ambulances, and they were healed. In time, I began to care less about what others might think, and instead, focused on what God thought of me. These two strategies helped me get past the fear and doubt that had blocked my progress.

You must be vigilant about what enters your mind. The books you read, the conversations you entertain, the media you consume—all of it shapes your mental terrain. A steady diet of doubt, fear, and cynicism will erode your readiness long before the enemy makes his move. Guarding your mind does not mean living in isolation. It's being intentional about what voices you allow to speak into your thought life. Every input is a seed. The fruit it bears shows whether it was wise to plant it.

Mental preparedness is not a one-time event. It is a daily practice with a beginning and an end. I start each morning by asking a simple question: What is God saying to me today? That question sets the orientation of my mind before the day's pressures have a chance to set it for me. Sometimes the answer comes through a dream I had overnight. Sometimes it comes as a quiet impression while I'm making coffee. The point is not to receive a spectacular revelation every morning. It's beginning the day by listening to God rather than hearing the noise of the world.

The other end of the day matters just as much. Many people get by on three or four hours of sleep, feel mentally drained, and operate at diminished capacity. Fear, anxiety, and worry are not just emotions. They are spirits that are quite happy to keep you awake. I began a practice each night of addressing that directly—telling spirits of fear, anxiety, and worry to leave, and then asking God to bring His presence for peace. The change was immediate. Some mornings I'd wake up reluctant to get out of bed, not from exhaustion but from a deep rest that feels almost like being glued to the floor in a worship service. I'm not promising that this will resolve every sleep problem—some cases of insomnia have metabolic or neurological causes—but for those whose sleeplessness comes from a mind that won't be quiet, the combination of commanding anxious spirits to leave and inviting God's peace in is worth trying.

These two bookends—a morning question and an evening clearing—are not complicated disciplines. They don't require time in a prayer closet or an elaborate routine. They're simply the practice of beginning and ending the day with your mind oriented toward God rather than toward whatever the enemy or the world is broadcasting. Do this consistently, and your mind will be hard to rattle, quick to find peace, and focused under pressure.

In battle, there will be chaos, but the prepared mind remains steady. It remembers the last clear word from the Commander. It holds fast until help arrives. It refuses to surrender ground. And in that steadiness, victory takes shape, because your thoughts are anchored in eternity.

CHAPTER TWENTY-SEVEN

Rest as Warfare

TODAY, OUR CULTURE VALUES CONSTANT activity. Our productivity is rewarded, and there is always pressure to do more. Many people believe that the more they accomplish, the more valuable they are. Rest can be viewed as laziness. God's kingdom views rest differently. Rest is not just a break from work or a luxury for those who can afford it. When God instructed Israel to observe the Sabbath, He did not give them a pointless tradition. He taught them to reject the mindset they learned in Egypt, where their worth was measured by what they produced.

For four hundred years, the Israelites lived as slaves in Egypt. Their value was determined by how much they produced. They were forced to make bricks without straw and were not allowed to rest unless it served Pharaoh's purposes. Their identity was tied to their labor. (The reader might take a moment and ask if their identity is in some way connected to their labor presently.)

When God brought the Israelites out of Egypt, He gave them a command that was unfamiliar to them: He told them to rest. By commanding them to rest, He reminded them that their identity was not based on their productivity, but on their relationship with Him.

Rest is not simply a break from work; it is a spiritual practice that opposes the mindset of the world and the schemes of the enemy. When you choose to rest, you reject the idea that your value comes from your activity. Rest reminds you that you are God's child, not just a worker who serves a system. It allows time for God to work in your mind and help you identify areas where you've been driven by unhealthy pressure or a need to prove yourself. Sometimes what we call dedication is, in fact, a form of bondage. Rest exposes these deceptive beliefs and helps us realign our priorities.

Jesus often withdrew from crowds to pray, even when people wanted more of His time. He did not measure success by activity or by meeting every demand. He prioritized His relationship with the Father, and time is the commodity of relationships.

The Sabbath was not meant to be a burdensome rule. Jesus said, "The Sabbath was made for man, not man for the Sabbath" (Mark 2:27). God gave the Sabbath as a gift to benefit us. Just as a soldier cannot fight without rest, we also need time to recover. Rest is necessary for maintaining spiritual and physical health.

Observing the Sabbath today does not require special rituals or ceremonies and is not tied to any particular day of the week. We are free to observe a day of rest on whatever day we choose. What matters is setting aside intentional time to commune with God.

In the same way, some think one day is more holy than another day, while others think every day is alike. You should each be fully convinced that whichever day you choose is acceptable. Those who worship the Lord on a special day do it to honor him. Those who eat any kind of food do so to honor the Lord, since they give thanks to God before eating. And those who refuse to eat certain foods also want to please the Lord and give thanks to God.
ROM 14:5-6 (NLT)

If you struggle to rest, it may be a sign of a deeper issue. Pushing yourself to keep working because you fear what will happen if you stop, or using busyness to avoid time with God, may be a symptom of incorrect priorities. A voice that demands constant work is not from God. Establish a time of rest as a personal boundary, and make it reasonable. When you rest and someone objects, ask them why. Then rest anyway. Their opinion about rest is their problem, not yours.

So far, we've discussed physical rest, but there is another aspect to consider. Rest is also a mindset. It's a perspective on life where peace dominates. Let me provide an illustration: When I worked as a paramedic, the scenes I responded to were generally chaotic. Emotions are contagious, and people often take their emotional cues from someone in uniform. There I was, standing in blood, trying to save someone's life, and the victim's wife was an emotional wreck. She looked at me and saw that I wasn't panicking. I was calm. My peace conveyed to her an unspoken message: she didn't need to panic. She calmed down, and her family members followed her lead. My peace about the situation helped others to be at peace. Inner peace can be thought of as rest. In the midst of a frantic scene, where I needed to stop the bleeding, start an IV, and get my patient to the hospital as soon as possible, I had many things to do, but I did them mentally, from a place of rest. This is the attitude Jesus had when He slept in the bow of the boat during the storm. It's why Mary was commended by Him while her sister Martha was chided over her inability to rest. Rest, in this sense, is not the absence of activity. It's an attitude. And that brings us to a related principle.

Silence in relationships can be a sign of trouble. When someone has crossed one of my boundaries, I may become silent, at least initially. In time, I will get their attention and address the matter. But silence is not always a harbinger of trouble. If you feel uncomfortable with silence in the presence of someone you know well and care deeply about, it may be a sign of insecurity. Do you continually need affirmation? One thing I love about my wife is that we can go for hours without saying a word, and neither of us feels a need to break the silence. I know Denise loves me, and she knows I love her, even during times of silence. Security in a relationship is sometimes marked by periods of silence. Silence is another form of rest. When you trust that the other person wants the best for you, there is no need for constant chatter. Choosing to rest—whether physically or emotionally—is an act of faith. It is knowing that your value does not come from constant work, and does not require continual affirmation. It is trusting that you are loved.

CHAPTER TWENTY-EIGHT

Reclaiming Wonder

THAT TRUST—THE SETTLED KNOWLEDGE THAT you are loved—is where wonder lives. A soul at rest is a soul that can be surprised by God again.

The kingdom of God is supernatural in all that it does. God works miracles through humans like you and me, but it is His Spirit connected to our spirit that makes the miraculous possible. When the spiritual dimension invades the natural realm, it creates a sense of awe. I can't speak for you, but the thing that compels me each day is a sense of wonder over the fact that the Creator of the universe chose to partner with me. Spiritual warfare isn't confined to violent confrontations with demons or principalities. It also takes place in the quiet moments when we are alone with our thoughts, and our sense of awe begins to fade. The enemy knows that wonder is a strong motivational force. If he cannot sabotage your calling directly, he will wear down your sense of wonder. Millions of believers who were once captivated by God's supernatural work returned to their previous patterns of thinking after losing their sense of wonder.

Wonder is not a luxury reserved for moments of leisure; it is oxygen for the soul. It is that childlike awareness that there is always more—more than we see, more than we understand, more than we can dream of. It is the unguarded posture that says, "I do not have to understand this moment. I only need to behold it." Wonder disarms cynicism, silences fear, and stretches our faith. Where wonder is alive, joy is quickened. And where joy lives, strength is reborn. The joy of the Lord is not ornamental—it is essential to our survival, and it is why the enemy wages relentless campaigns to rob our sense of wonder. A soul absorbed in awe stays spiritually sharp, yet tender and loving—resilient and receptive.

Beauty is often viewed as a superficial quality that is unworthy of serious consideration. However, in God's kingdom, beauty has a purpose. It is one way in which God communicates with us. Beauty reminds us of His glory, His wisdom, and goodness. It's easy to become so focused on our struggles that we stop noticing beauty. We become tired and lose sight of what we are fighting for. Intentionally focusing on the beauty of creation helps us remember God's original design and His promise to restore all things.

Stillness is the doorway through which beauty enters the soul. It is not idleness but an intentional pause, a sacred silence during which God is allowed to be larger than the world in which we dwell. Psalm 46:10 does not say, "Hurry and know that I am God." It says, "Be still." Some truths reveal themselves only in the absence of motion. In stillness, the noise fades, and our ears catch melodies we had forgotten—songs and strategies, beauty and battle plans, the heartbeat of the Father conveying His love alongside His marching orders. David wrote the psalms in stillness. Elijah heard the still small voice in the quiet of a cave.

Reclaiming wonder is a deliberate act. It's stepping outside and letting creation recalibrate your soul—letting a sunset and a placid pond remind you of truths too deep for words. It's choosing silence over the hum of headlines and notifications, giving your nervous system a chance to breathe. It's walking without a destination, eating without distraction, writing, drawing, singing, building—not to impress anyone, but simply to reveal the treasure God has placed inside an earthen vessel. It is surrounding yourself with beauty, whether by lighting a candle, placing flowers in a jar, hanging a painting, or reading a poem. These are not shallow indulgences; they are acts of hope. It is learning once more how to gaze—not glancing, not scanning, but beholding with lingering attention—a shooting star, a page of scripture, or the face of someone you love.

When we reclaim wonder, something in us begins to heal. Wonder repairs what worry corrodes. It pulls us out of survival mode and back into sacred awareness. It restores the part of us that can believe even without full understanding—not because we have the answers, but because we have seen enough to trust the One who does. And when the eyes of the heart open again, we discover that God has been there all along, waiting not to issue a new command, but to sit with us in the grass and whisper, "Isn't this beautiful? I made it for you."

You are not only a warrior; you are a soul, a heart, a child of wonder. And wonder is part of your inheritance. So rest. Be still. And look again with awe.

CHAPTER TWENTY-NINE

Growing into New Assignments

I BECAME A BELIEVER IN the year 2000. At the time, I was in the middle of a long and grinding battle with supervisors at work. For seven years, my assignment—though I wouldn't have called it that—was to learn the Bible. Nothing supernatural happened. I attended church each week, read scripture daily, and listened to Bible studies whenever I could. That was it. It didn't feel like training. It felt like waiting.

That changed in 2007, when I met Denise. When we married, we started attending a Charismatic congregation. For the first time, I heard people singing in tongues. Each week, prophets delivered words to individuals in the room. It was entirely new to me, and I was fascinated. In 2008, the dreams began, and God asked me to pray for my patients. I had no faith for it and no experience. Nine months passed before I saw anyone healed. During that season, I was learning to receive visions, interpret dreams, and deliver prophetic words—each requiring its own cycle of study, practice, and stumbling through mistakes before anything resembling proficiency arrived.

In 2014, after years of seeing people healed physically, I asked God whether there was a way to heal mental illness. Dreams came. Over the next several years, I read everything I could find on emotional healing and began developing an approach—eventually arriving at one that could be completed during a ten-minute ambulance ride.

In 2016, God gave me a new assignment. He asked me to begin reporting on political corruption. I had no interest in politics at the time and knew next to nothing about it. But I had learned by then that when God gives an assignment, the learning comes with it. And learn, I did.

I've shared all of this to make a single point: new assignments require us to grow. Each season brought a different set of skills, a different body of knowledge, a different kind of obedience. None of it arrived ready-made. The recruit who was learning the Bible in 2000 was not the same person God commissioned to pray for patients in 2008, and neither of them was ready for what came in 2014 or 2016.

The growth that preceded each assignment was not incidental. It was a necessary part of the process. I had to learn the Bible to understand God's plan for healing. Then, I had to experience people leaving my ambulance unhealed before I would ask about emotional healing, which, as it turns out, is the very reason why many people are not physically healed through prayer. I had to learn to see visions before I could sense what God was saying about how a person's medical condition could be healed or how the trauma they had suffered should be resolved. One assignment led to the next, which led to the next. Ignoring an assignment God has given you virtually guarantees that you will not complete the ones that follow, because the later ones require knowledge or skill that you presently lack. People often ask why the ministry they dream of has not materialized. In most cases, it is because of unfinished assignments.

God does not give a new recruit command of a battalion. He doesn't hand the keys to someone who hasn't yet learned to drive. He starts small, watches how you steward what you've been given, and expands your responsibility in proportion to your faithfulness. Even Jesus, though fully divine, learned obedience through suffering. The pattern is consistent throughout scripture: preparation precedes deployment.

Those in transition often sense the end of one season without yet seeing the door to the next. Assignments feel completed, but no new orders have arrived. Dreams shift, burdens change, relationships are pruned. These in-between spaces are uncomfortable. They are also necessary. God is more interested in what He is forming in you than in what He is giving you. The two are connected, but the second depends on the first.

If you intend to fulfill your destiny and partner with God, there is no alternative to growth. The kingdom only expands to the extent that we are willing to be stretched. Make the adjustments. Learn the skills. Practice until you can do them well. Trust that every season of preparation—even the ones that feel like waiting—is moving you toward the next thing He has in mind.

CHAPTER THIRTY

Divine Transfer Orders

IN THE MILITARY, ORDERS ARE given by those in authority. There is no discussion or debate about it. The instruction is clear: report to your new assignment. The reasons behind the decision are not always explained, but the soldier follows the command. God often directs us in a similar way. Sometimes, He tells us to leave our current assignment and move to a new one with little warning or explanation. You may be faithfully serving where He placed you, and then sense that it is time to move on. Sometimes the next step is clear, but other times, you may not know exactly where you are going. In either case, God asks us to obey before we have all the details.

The Bible gives us many examples of this kind of transition. Abraham was told to leave his home and go to a land he did not know. Joseph went from prison to a position of authority in a single day. Elijah moved from hiding by a brook to standing before a king. Paul planned to preach in Asia, but God redirected him to Macedonia through a vision. In each situation, God gave enough instruction to take the next step, but not enough information to remove the need for faith. Often, the first sign that a change is coming is a sense of restlessness or noticing that what once worked well now feels difficult or closed.

As discussed in the previous chapter, assignments can be issued in the same time frame. I've worked on many assignments that overlapped. But other times, a new assignment can only be started by ending the one you're presently working on. In my experience, a sign that God may be preparing you for a new assignment is a gradual loss of interest or passion for your current one. The place or role you once felt called to may no longer feel the same. Opportunities may decrease, and your prayers for that sphere may feel less effective. At the same time, you may feel drawn to new people, places, or causes, sometimes through dreams or persistent thoughts. Occasionally, the Holy Spirit will speak clearly about the change. Even if you do not know exactly what is next, you sense that God is leading you in a new direction.

How you leave an assignment is important. It is best to confirm that God is moving you, rather than leaving out of frustration, presumption, or exhaustion. Once confirmation is received, we do not simply abandon our present responsibilities; we return them to God with care. Pray for the people and the work you are leaving behind, and ask God to bless the next person who will take your place. Sometimes, leaving is difficult and feels like saying goodbye to family. Even Paul grieved when he left the churches he started. Letting go is not failure; it is following God's direction. Staying out too long, out of habit or uncertainty, can hinder both you and those you serve. When your assignment is finished, release it to God and let Him take the responsibility from you.

When you begin a new assignment, it may feel unfamiliar or uncomfortable at first. Like Abraham, you may not fully understand where God is leading you until you are there. You might not have the same influence or recognition you had in the past. Try to approach the new situation with humility and a willingness to learn. Ask God to show you how things work in this new place, and to reveal the people He has prepared to help you. Remember that the methods that worked before may not be effective here. Some assignments are for planting seeds, preparing the ground, or building foundations, not just for seeing immediate results.

Divine transfer orders do not always make sense in the moment. They may come in the middle of what looks like success, when the work seems unfinished. But heaven's intelligence sees further than we do. The Commander might be moving you to prevent burnout, to open space for another to step in, or to protect you from unseen danger.

Sometimes the new sphere God leads you to feels like a wilderness. Moses spent forty years in the desert herding sheep before leading Israel. Elijah hid in a cave. Jesus was led by the Spirit into the desert to be tested. These seasons are not the end of your journey. God uses them to prepare and strengthen you for what is coming next.

When God gives you a new direction, do not hold on to the past. Thank Him for what He has done in your previous assignment, and be willing to move forward in obedience. Trust that His timing is right, even if it interrupts your plans.

The prophet Isaiah wrote, "Forget the former things; do not dwell on the past. See, I am doing a new thing." God is always leading us forward. New opportunities and responsibilities are ahead. Stay sharp. Stay under orders. The next battlefield is already waiting for your arrival.

CHAPTER THIRTY-ONE

Inheritance and Legacy

SOME DIVINE ASSIGNMENTS ARE TEMPORARY. They last for a season, are given for a specific purpose, or are designed to create a fleeting moment of impact. Other assignments are intended to last for generations. There is a kind of authority that is not based on your destination, but on what you are called to establish. This authority shapes the spiritual environment of a neighborhood, a family, or a ministry, and its effects remain for those who come after you. I refer to this as spiritual inheritance.

A spiritual inheritance begins when God gives you an assignment to build something that will continue after you are gone. This is not learning a new skill or winning a particular battle. It's establishing a place where God's presence remains for generations to come. Soldiers may fight for victory, but those who build for the future—founders, fathers, and mothers—work to leave a legacy.

An assignment is something you carry out because you've been given specific instructions. It is temporary, often strategic, and sometimes has a clear endpoint. Inheritance, on the other hand, is based on a covenant. It is a long-term responsibility that God entrusts to you and to those who come after you. It can be a physical or spiritual territory, and God intends for it to grow and flourish over time. When God brought Israel into the Promised Land, He told them it was not like Egypt, but a land He Himself would care for over generations. Your inheritance is something God chooses, oversees, and expects to multiply through your stewardship.

The Bible gives us many examples of spiritual inheritance. Abraham was promised that his descendants would become a great nation and inherit a land. His responsibility was to obey God, even though he did not see the complete fulfillment of the promise in his lifetime. His faith established a covenant that would last forever. David fought many battles and won victories, but his most important legacy was establishing worship in Israel and preparing for the building of the temple, which he did not live to see. God promised David that his descendants would rule, a promise fulfilled in Jesus. Paul started many churches, but his greatest inheritance was the people he mentored, like Timothy and Titus, who continued his work after he was gone.

When God calls you to build a legacy, your focus will shift. You will not only be concerned with immediate results, but with creating something that will last after you are gone. Your prayers will be directed toward lasting change. You'll invest in people who can continue the work, rather than just seeking help for the present moment.

If God gives you the seed of an inheritance, you are responsible to care for it. You may need to train and disciple others so that the work continues after you are gone. You must protect what God has entrusted to you, because the enemy will try to destroy or corrupt it.

One reason I write books is to build a legacy. Of course, I want to train and equip the saints of my own generation. But long after I join the great cloud of witnesses, someone will find this book, and it will impact their life. Their changed life may change the lives of others hundreds of years from now. That's legacy.

The enemy hates inheritance. Temporary assignments may annoy him, but generational legacies threaten the kingdom of darkness itself. It's why Jezebel silenced the prophets who raised up sons, why Pharaoh and Herod turned their wrath on infants. Satan knows that if he can stop legacy, he can halt the advance of God's kingdom. So, when you labor for inheritance, expect resistance—delays that test your patience, discouragement over small beginnings, assaults against your character, and attacks meant to fracture the relationships that can multiply your effectiveness. Yet none of this should deter you. You are not just passing through. You are planting seeds in eternity.

Your legacy is not limited to traditional ministry. It could be a house church that changes a neighborhood, a school that changes how children learn, or a business that influences an entire industry. For example, the U.S. Department of Justice created a new fraud division after one person exposed large-scale fraud against the government. Sometimes, your inheritance is not a new organization or system, but the people you have trained—spiritual sons and daughters who carry your values and authority into places you may never go.

When the Israelites had finally crossed over the Jordan River, God told them to build a pile of stones as a memorial.

> *Now the people came up from the Jordan on the tenth day of the first month, and they camped in Gilgal on the east border of Jericho. And those twelve stones which they took out of the Jordan, Joshua set up in Gilgal. Then he spoke to the children of Israel, saying: "When your children ask their fathers in time to come, saying, 'What are these stones?' then you shall let your children know, saying, 'Israel crossed over this Jordan on dry land'; for the Lord your God dried up the waters of the Jordan before you until you had crossed over, as the Lord your God did to the Red Sea, which He dried up before us until we had crossed over, that all the peoples of the earth may know the hand of the Lord, that it is mighty, that you may fear the Lord your God forever."*
> JOSH 4:19-24

Proverbs says a good man leaves an inheritance to his children's children. Your descendants will build on the ground you take.

CHAPTER THIRTY-TWO

Gatekeeping in Your Neighborhood

A FRIEND OF MINE NAMED Al Mack, who writes under the pseudonym Northwest Prophetic, tells a story that illustrates what neighborhood-level jurisdiction looks like in practice.

When Al and his family moved into a new home, they soon discovered that there were three drug dealers operating on their block. He went to the authorities, who explained the standards of evidence required before the police could act. He went to the neighbors, who shook their heads. Then he went to God—and by his own account, he mostly whined.

God let him vent. Then came a question: So, what are you going to do about it?

That stopped him. He asked what he could do, and God gave him specific prayer strategies—not legal strategies, not social ones, but spiritual ones. The image God gave him was that of a gatekeeper, the one who decides what enters and what does not. He was instructed to establish spiritual gates at the entrances to his neighborhood and to make a declaration over them: welcome the Holy Spirit, welcome the rightful residents and their guests, and bar everything else.

He did it in the middle of the night because he didn't want anyone calling the police on him. Within 30 days, all three drug dealers were gone. The house across the street was sold to a family with a daughter the same age as his. The other two houses were soon remodeled. He describes it as the most precisely answered prayer he had ever seen.

Then, a neighbor invited a woman to move in next door. She brought two wolves, which were permitted by law, he was told, though no agency thought they belonged in a residential neighborhood. When they lunged at his daughter and nearly injured her, he confronted the neighbor, who responded with rage and a declaration that the wolves were not leaving, not ever.

Al prayed again. God's response came faster this time: You're my representative here. What's your decision?

He didn't have a theology that cleanly answered the question, but he had already been given a principle. He said the wolves had to go—and he knew as he said it that he was speaking with the authority of a judge issuing a decree.

That weekend, the neighbor took the wolf enclosure apart himself, loaded everything into his truck, and moved out. No explanation. They were never seen again.

Al closes the account with a note of honest qualification. A pornography shop closed after he made declarations over it, only to be replaced by another one. A pagan worship center closed, then reopened a couple of blocks away. Both eventually closed for good, but the path to victory was not clean or immediate.

His conclusions were modest and practical. God delegates authority to His representatives in a given area. He takes that delegated authority seriously. And those who have been granted it would do well to exercise it for good purpose, within the bounds of what they have been assigned.

That last point is the one worth further discussion. Al's authority extended for a few blocks. He was not commissioned to pray over the city at this time. He had been placed in a specific neighborhood, and that placement was his jurisdiction. The results came when he acted within that boundary, in obedience to specific instruction, rather than from ambition to do something on a larger scale.

It is a small-scale story, which is exactly what makes it useful. Most warfare doesn't happen at the level of states and nations. It happens on a street, in a neighborhood, on a block where someone has been placed and is willing to ask what God wants them to do about it.

Engaging Territorial Spirits

WHY DO SOME NATIONS LANGUISH in economic poverty despite generations of effort to build prosperity? Why does a city like Washington D.C. carry a tradition of both liberty and a deep culture of corruption? Why have certain regions of the world remained resistant to the most basic principles of human dignity—producing cycles of cannibalism, human sacrifice, and tribal violence that persist despite centuries of missionary work, education, and development? Sociological explanations account for some of it. But not all of it. The biblical answer is that some of these patterns are not merely human constructs. They are maintained by spiritual powers assigned to specific territories.

Scripture calls them principalities, powers, and rulers of darkness. They are not demons who torment individuals. They operate at a different level entirely, shaping the laws, institutions, ideologies, and cultural assumptions of entire regions. In the book of Daniel, the "prince of

Persia" delayed the answer to Daniel's prayers for twenty-one days until Michael the archangel intervened. This was not a human official. It was a spiritual power with jurisdictional authority over a geopolitical region, actively resisting God's purposes.

The Gospels show the same pattern. When Jesus cast the legion of demons from the Gadarene man, the spirits begged not to be sent out of their region. They knew their territory and were fighting to keep it. Yet notice that Jesus delivered the man without launching a direct campaign against the spirits ruling the area. And Paul, whose preaching so disrupted the idol trade in Ephesus that the silversmiths rioted, never marched against the temple of Artemis. He preached truth, and the power of the gospel dismantled the stronghold from the inside. Both are instructive. The goal is not confrontation for its own sake. It is the displacement of darkness by the presence of God.

Territorial spirits are usually identified not by sensing them directly, but by the patterns they leave—a city with cycles of violence; a nation where corruption regenerates no matter who takes power; a region where revival consistently stalls; or a culture where certain sins run like a current through generation after generation. When you see these patterns, the right question is not only what spirit is present, but what has given it legal access to remain—bloodshed, idolatry, broken covenants, or the long-term absence of repentance and prayer.

If God commissions you to engage at this level, preparation is mandatory. Your own life and the lives of those around you must be clean. Unconfessed sin is a point of access the enemy will exploit. Repentance on behalf of the land, as Daniel modeled, is often required. Covenants that empower the territorial spirit must be identified and renounced. And when darkness is displaced, something must fill the void—worship, ministry, truth, and a culture that establishes the presence of God in territory that was previously conceded to the enemy.

The story of Potosi, Bolivia, illustrates what territorial warfare looks like when every element is in order—the preparation, the assignment, the spiritual mapping, and the outcome that follows obedience. Fernando Orihuela, an apostolic leader from La Paz, shares the account in Ana Mendez Ferrell's book *Regions of Captivity*.

Potosi sits at over 13,000 feet above sea level in the Bolivian highlands. In the sixteenth century, Spanish conquistadors discovered that the mountain above the city contained one of the richest silver deposits in history. By 1650, Potosi had become the largest city in the Americas—larger than London or Paris—with its silver funding the Spanish empire and flowing across Europe. The price of that wealth was measured in human lives. Historians estimate that over 350 years, approximately twelve million men died extracting silver from those mines. Workers were forced to chew coca leaves to survive the altitude and the brutal conditions, producing addiction, physical ruin, and shortened lives. The blood of millions soaked the mountain and the soil around it. Well into the twentieth century, Potosi had a life expectancy below 47 years and was the only city in Bolivia with negative population growth.

One practice took root in the mines and persisted for generations: the worship of a figure called "the Uncle," a representation of the devil, to whom offerings were regularly made. The theology behind it was simple—the miners believed the devil owned the mountain and its riches. That covenant, established in blood and sustained through generations of ritual, gave the enemy legal ground on which to stand. Christianity had made almost no inroads despite more than a century of missionary work. The churches that existed were small and divided. Occult practices were common. Poverty was embedded in the culture.

Orihuela began working toward city transformation in Potosi in the mid-1990s. Over five years, he and a small team made regular visits, conducting spiritual mapping—studying the city's history, visiting museums, entering the mines, tracing the roots of what had taken hold of the place. The work was slow and the opposition considerable. Even personal deliverance ministry in Potosi required unusual effort.

In early 2001, Orihuela connected with Ana Mendez Ferrell and a small team of intercessors. Shortly after arriving in Potosi, Ferrell gathered the group for intercession. What followed, by Orihuela's account, was unlike anything he had previously experienced. Over three hours, the team found themselves drawn into a spiritual revelation of the city's condition—seeing, as he describes it, the structures of darkness that had held it captive for generations. They identified the territorial spirit holding the city and discerned that its authority had been established through the blood of the millions who died in those mines. Two other principalities appeared to the intercessors as guardians of that throne, corresponding to the twin realities that had defined Potosi's history: the spirits of Mammon and Death.

The intercession continued across three sessions. In each one, the team reported breakthroughs, with covenants being broken and structures displaced. Only five people were present for the high-level warfare. The evangelistic mobilization that followed involved more than 400 workers going door to door across the city.

In 10 days of evangelism, 40,790 people made decisions for Christ. On the second day alone, the team ran out of the 17,000 decision cards they had prepared. People were coming to Christ after midnight in temperatures of minus 11 degrees Celsius—inmates, city officials, students, and entire farming communities.

The longer-term consequences were equally striking. Within three months, the president of Bolivia—whose administration had been marked by corruption—resigned and died shortly afterward of a terminal illness. The political parties that had dominated the country for fifty years collapsed. Within three years, Potosi had risen to second in the nation for economic and investment projections. The practice of using children as mine laborers was banned by law.

Orihuela's summary is an understatement: "The invisible government fell. The visible government falls."

This is what it looks like when territorial warfare is done correctly—years of preparation, spiritual mapping that identifies the actual legal ground the enemy is standing on, a small team operating within clearly defined assignments, intercession that addresses specific covenants and principalities, and the displacement of darkness filled immediately with the presence of God through prayer, worship, and the gospel. The outcome was not manufactured. It followed from obedience.

Engaging territorial spirits is not something you do because you sense a dark presence or feel strongly about an issue. Sensing is not commissioning. The authority to act at this level comes from a specific assignment from God, confirmed through prayer, scripture, and the counsel of mature believers who can see the field of battle with you. When the assignment is clear, act. When it is not, intercede—and trust that God is raising up those He has commissioned to take back that ground.

Cleansing the Land

BREAKING THE ENEMY'S OCCUPATION OF a territory is one thing. Reclaiming and redeeming the land that was corrupted by evil is another. When territorial spirits are displaced, the work has not ended—it has only begun. The victory is incomplete until the land itself is washed clean, its spiritual wounds healed, and a solid, new foundation has been established.

Throughout scripture, land is never portrayed as a passive backdrop on which human events unfold. It remembers. It bears witness. It records the covenants made upon it, the blood shed into it, and the sins committed on its surface. These imprints remain as spiritual residue, and unless they are dealt with, they continue to speak. When God entrusts us with new territory, whether it be a city block, a mountain valley, or an institutional sphere, we cannot simply occupy it without first cleansing the ground beneath our feet.

Cain learned this truth in the earliest chapters of Genesis. When his brother's blood spilled into the earth, God did not say it was forgotten. He said it cried out from the ground for justice. The voice of that blood was not metaphorical; it was a testimony embedded in the soil itself, demanding an answer. Later, when the Lord warned Israel about the land of Canaan, He was not speaking in abstract moral terms. The soil had been defiled by generations of idolatry, perversion, and human sacrifice, and it would "vomit out" those who continued to pollute it. The principle is clear: certain sins saturate the ground until even creation cannot bear them. Daniel understood this as well when he fell on his knees and repented, not only for his own failings, but for the sins of an entire nation. His confession was priestly intercession, an appeal to God for the cleansing of both people and land.

When territory is reclaimed, the lingering effects of what took place there cannot be ignored. Bloodshed leaves a stain, whether it came through murder, war, or hidden violence. Idolatry weaves invisible chains through false worship, occult rituals, and generational dedications. Sexual perversion corrupts both individuals and the culture around them. Injustice leaves scars where slavery, exploitation, and corruption took root. Even the breaking of solemn agreements—marriages, treaties, covenants—can fracture the spiritual foundation of a location. Defilement gives legal ground to the powers of darkness, and even when the strongman has been bound, the imprint of his rule can remain, ready to draw him back unless the breach is closed.

The process of cleansing the land begins with revelation. The Spirit of God often points to the root of a defilement through unexpected means—a historical record that surfaces at the right moment, a prophetic dream that exposes forgotten events, a word of knowledge that brings hidden things to light, the confession of someone who participated in the sin. These revelations are not given for curiosity's sake; they are intelligence for a legal proceeding. They allow us to bring the matter before God's court and stand in the gap on behalf of the land.

Intercessory repentance is the next act. Like Daniel, we do not need to pretend the guilt is ours, but we take the posture of one who identifies with the people and land, confessing the wrongs committed and appealing for mercy. In prayer, we acknowledge the specific sins that gave the enemy a foothold, and we ask the Lord to forgive and remove the record of those charges from the land's history. We then address the covenants and agreements that tied the ground to darkness. In the authority of Jesus, we cancel every ungodly vow, dedication, sacrifice, and ritual. We declare that ownership has been transferred—this land no longer belongs to the powers of darkness, but to the Lord.

Often the Spirit will lead an intercessor in a physical act of consecration. Oil, water, or wine may be poured onto the ground as a prophetic seal, marking it as holy. Words are spoken aloud as a legal declaration: this ground is now a dwelling place for the presence of God, dedicated to righteousness and kingdom purposes. When we speak as the Spirit leads, our words carry the authority of heaven. Scripture is filled with such acts—Jacob anointing the stone at Bethel, priests sprinkling oil and blood in the tabernacle, kings rededicating the temple after seasons of defilement. These outward actions mirror the invisible work taking place in the spirit realm.

Once the land is cleansed, it must not remain empty. After cleansing, the ground must be filled with blessing, worship, prayer, and righteous activity. Worship, intercession, declarations of God's purpose, and the visible presence of God's people keep the door closed to the enemy and establish a new spiritual climate. This is not elaborate or highly visible work. I have prayed over parking lots and alleys filled with trash. The invisibility is appropriate. What matters is obedience to what the Spirit shows you, not the production value of how it looks.

History bears witness to what happens when land is cleansed. The Welsh Revival followed prayers of repentance for generations of spiritual apathy. In the Hebrides, fasting and confession preceded an outpouring that transformed entire communities. Even the humble beginnings of the Azusa Street Revival were marked by the Spirit sweeping through a small home, displacing decades of spiritual stagnation in Los Angeles. In each case, the revival was not only personal—it was territorial. The land itself became an altar.

Yet we must not be naïve. When the legal eviction of darkness begins, the enemy pushes back. Retaliation may take the form of a sudden disruption, a natural disaster, a public scandal, or a personal failure.

This is not the time to retreat in fear, but to stand on the legal ground established by the blood of Jesus. The land is the Lord's, and no weapon formed against His purposes will stand. When opposition escalates, it is wise to call in reinforcements. Land cleansing is rarely a solo mission; it is the work of teams, families, and spiritual communities moving in one accord.

The goal is not simply to remove darkness but to prepare the land for inheritance. Cleansed ground becomes a place where Christ is enthroned, and His plan takes shape. God told Joshua, "Every place where you set your foot, I will give you." That promise still stands. We walk our neighborhoods with prayer. We lay hands on buildings and pray in parking lots and doorways. We repent for what was done on the ground we now occupy, and we fill the atmosphere with worship and the presence of God's people. The land becomes what it was always meant to be—a dwelling place for Him.

CHAPTER THIRTY-FIVE

Intercessory Warfare

NOT ALL PRAYER IS THE same, and understanding the differences between the various forms of prayer is important before we continue. Supplication is intimate communication with God—laying your heart before Him, asking, receiving, resting in His presence. Petition is bringing specific requests before God and trusting Him to act. Some petitions are submitted in the court of heaven as a request for mercy from the Judge. Healing prayer is an exercise of authority—commanding sickness, evil spirits, or infirmity to leave, rather than asking God to do something He has already commissioned you to do. Praying in tongues bypasses the natural mind entirely, allowing the Holy Spirit to pray through you with a precision not attainable on your own. Intercession is prayer on behalf of others, and when it rises to the level of warfare, it involves sustained, deliberate engagement against specific spiritual opposition. Each form of prayer has its place. A mature prayer life draws on all of them.

Intercessory warfare addresses spiritual opposition directly. In contrast to quiet devotional prayer, intercession involves persistent, focused engagement that establishes God's will in the face of resistance. It is not simply asking God to intervene. It is actively enforcing the victory of Christ in areas where the enemy has built a stronghold. In the days of Ezekiel, God looked for someone to stand in the gap for the land. Intercessors take that role, positioning themselves between people or regions under threat and the enemy's attacks, and persisting until the breakthrough comes.

Intercessory warfare can take several forms depending on what the situation requires. Sometimes it resembles a legal proceeding—bringing God's promises before Him, appealing to His justice and mercy on behalf of another. Other times, it is direct engagement: speaking to the opposition, declaring God's truth, and commanding the enemy to depart. A good example of this type of warfare is found in *The Two Towers* scene where Gandalf confronts the Balrog. Sometimes it flows from deep intimacy, where you are listening more than speaking, praying according to what God is showing you in the moment, rather than what you already know.

The tools of warfare are spiritual. The Word of God carries power that overcomes resistance. The blood of Jesus removes guilt, cancels accusations, and gives us confidence to pray. Praise and worship shift the atmosphere and establish God's presence in contested ground. And when words fail, the Holy Spirit intercedes through us in ways that exceed our understanding or ability—this is where praying in tongues is the weapon of choice.

Effective intercessory warfare begins with a clear sense of assignment. Authority flows from being sent, not from personal initiative or spiritual ambition. Once the assignment is confirmed, ask the Holy Spirit for intelligence: what is the enemy doing, what lies are being believed, what doors have been opened that need to be closed. This allows you to pray with precision rather than general spiritual effort. Examine your own life before engaging. Unconfessed sin and unresolved trauma give the enemy points of access that can be exploited in the middle of battle. And whenever possible, pray with others. Agreement multiplies effectiveness and provides covering when the fight is long.

Intercessory warfare can focus on an individual who needs to be freed from oppression or drawn back to God. It can focus on an institution, a region, or a culture steeped in spiritual darkness. It can address destructive patterns within a family line, or recover purposes that have been stolen or buried. Each situation calls for discernment about which approach fits—declaration, fasting, travail, confrontation, or quiet listening for the Spirit's direction.

The results are not always immediate. Sometimes you sense a shift in the room. Sometimes the evidence arrives days or weeks later. You may never see the outcome this side of eternity. But no Spirit-led prayer is wasted. If God has given you a burden for a person, place, or situation, that burden is an invitation. Take your place. Pray with faith. Stay until the assignment is complete.

CHAPTER THIRTY-SIX

Worship as Warfare

WORSHIP IS NOT A GENRE of music. It is a spiritual practice with tangible effects in the invisible realm. When we worship in faith, we invite God's presence into our circumstances—and where His presence is, spiritual opposition loses its hold.

Now the Lord is the Spirit; and where the Spirit of the Lord is, there is liberty.
2 COR 3:17

Worship is more than expressing love for God; it is resistance to the influence of darkness. In the days of King Jehoshaphat, singers led the advance, praising God, and He acted on their behalf without their needing to engage in combat. The enemy's lines broke not by the clash of swords but under the sound of exaltation. This is the power of worship on the battlefield.

The effects of worship in spiritual conflict are not consistent with natural logic. I didn't understand the dynamics of worship when I first became a believer. What I've learned since is that worship replaces fear, confusion, and heaviness with faith, joy, and peace. We receive a garment of praise in exchange for the spirit of heaviness. Worship invites the manifest presence of God and the engagement of angels. If you want to stand in the presence of angels, find a good worship service. I've seen angels more often during worship than in any other setting.

Worship itself can cause demons to flee. When King David played for Saul, the tormenting spirit departed without David issuing a single command. The worship was the weapon.

Worship takes different forms depending on what the moment requires. Sometimes, it is simply fixing your attention on God's character and goodness—adoration that draws His presence into a difficult circumstance. At other times, it is a declaration of truth against lies. Both are warfare. The form matters less than the faith behind it.

Worship leaders carry more than a musical role. Their task is to help create an environment where God's presence can be experienced and His purposes accomplished. That requires integrity, sensitivity to the moment, and the ability to follow God's lead. Whether the moment calls for praise, lament, or declaration, an effective worship leader reads the room—and the spirit—and leads accordingly. Other leaders should be sensitive to the leading of the Spirit, too. I attended a church years ago where the pastor had enough sensitivity and humility to set aside his sermon and allow worship to continue for the entire meeting when God prompted him.

The effectiveness of public worship is shaped by what happens in private. David's public victory over Goliath grew from the years he spent alone, worshiping God in the fields while tending sheep and facing lions. What you cultivate in private, you carry onto the battlefield. If you want to change the atmosphere of a room or a region, begin by changing the atmosphere of your own life.

The enemy once stood in the presence of God and lost that place forever. When you worship, you are occupying ground he forfeited—declaring that you belong to God and that He rules here. Worship is not merely singing. It is a territorial statement.

When the fog of war descends, when uncertainty grips you, do not retreat. Let your voice be the trumpet that announces the Lord's arrival. Let your hands be lifted as a banner. Let your King be enthroned in the very place the enemy thought he ruled. And then—watch the walls fall, the chains break, and the glory of God flood the battlefield.

CHAPTER THIRTY-SEVEN

The Glory of God in Spiritual Warfare

THERE IS A DIMENSION OF God's presence that most teaching on spiritual warfare doesn't address. We speak of identity, authority, the name of Jesus, the blood of the Lamb, and of the Word of God. All of these are necessary and effective. But there is something else available to the believer that is less often discussed: the manifest presence of God, sometimes called His glory, operating as a direct force in the conflict itself.

To understand this concept, it helps to distinguish between two aspects of God's presence. In one sense, God is present everywhere. He is omniscient and aware of all things. Nothing escapes His notice. But there is a second aspect of His presence—what the Bible sometimes calls His glory, or manifest presence—that is not everywhere at once. It moves. It settles. It departs. It can fill a room or rest upon a person in a perceptible way that produces specific effects. This is the presence that inhabited the temple in Jerusalem, that descended on the disciples as tongues of fire at Pentecost, that rested on Jesus at His baptism, and remained there. It is what Peter's friends described when they said it felt as though a presence was moving through the streets of Jerusalem before they had seen a miracle.

The apostle Peter wrote that the Spirit of glory rests upon those who are reproached for the name of Christ (1 Pet. 4:14). Paul, writing to the Corinthians, connected the manifest presence of the Spirit to liberty: "Where the Spirit of the Lord is, there is freedom." Not the awareness that God exists—every demon has that—but the active manifestation of His presence displacing darkness. This is a different kind of engagement with the spiritual realm. Rather than directly confronting opposition, you welcome the presence of God into the situation and allow His glory to do what it does naturally—expose, displace, and transform.

What the Manifest Presence Does

The effects of God's manifest glory in a contested space are consistent across scripture and testimony. It heals—not because someone commands disease to leave, but because where God's glory is, sickness cannot remain. It shifts atmospheres—the quality of a room, a home, a region changes when the glory of God arrives. Heaviness lifts. Fear loses its grip. Confusion gives way to clarity. These are not mere metaphors. They are the operational effects of a presence that is stronger than any spiritual opposition.

God's glory also empowers intercessors. Many of the most effective intercessors I know don't begin their prayer time by immediately engaging the enemy. They begin by inviting God's presence. They ask Him to come, make room for His glory, and wait until they sense His nearness before speaking another word.

God's glory manifests in different ways depending on what's needed. When I operate in healing, I ask God to bring His presence for healing. Consider the implication of the following verse:

Now it happened on a certain day, as He was teaching, that there were Pharisees and teachers of the law sitting by, who had come

166

out of every town of Galilee, Judea, and Jerusalem. And the power of the Lord was present to heal them.
LUKE 5:17

When we are about to engage in warfare, we can ask God to bring His presence for revelation, if we need to know whether enemy structures are present or which tactics to use for a specific mission. If the issue involves fear or strife, ask God to bring His presence for peace. An intercessor who prays from within the manifest presence of God prays with a different authority than one who simply issues commands into the air. They are working directly with the power of God.

Inviting the Presence

Inviting God's glory must be practiced. I learned it gradually in the context of healing ministry, but I've come to understand that it applies equally to intercession and warfare. Before engaging in any spiritual activity, I ask God to bring His presence into the situation—specifically, the manifest presence related to the issue at hand. I usually sense His presence immediately. God's glory affects everyone differently. My wife feels a weighty presence upon her. I sway gently back and forth involuntarily. Some people feel tingling. Sometimes, God's glory manifests as gold dust that appears for a fleeting moment before dissipating.

The practical form of this can vary. It may begin with worship—an invitation for God to come. It may involve sitting in silence, expectant and attentive. It may be initiated by praying in tongues, allowing the Holy Spirit to align your mind and spirit with what heaven is doing. What matters is the intentionality—actively making space for His glory rather than proceeding immediately into warfare.

A Caution

God's manifest presence is not a tool. He is a Person, and His glory is an expression of who He is, not a resource to be deployed. Believers who treat the presence of God as a mechanical process will find that it becomes elusive. Relationship is central to everything we do, and ministry done in the absence of relationship is dead religion. What invites God's presence is the same thing that has always invited it: surrender, worship, humility, and a desire to know Him rather than use Him.

When the glory of God fills the battlefield, the enemy retreats. The safest place in any spiritual battle is the center of God's manifest presence. The believer who lives there is harder to dislodge than one who relies solely on authority and technique. Carry the glory. The enemy is defenseless against it.

CHAPTER THIRTY-EIGHT

The Court of Accusation

THE CONCEPT OF THE COURTS of heaven is not new, although the terminology may be unfamiliar to some. The Bible contains several examples of legal proceedings in heaven, such as Job's trial before the divine council, and Zechariah's vision of Joshua the high priest being accused by Satan. Unlike human courts, which are often bureaucratic and impersonal, the courts of heaven operate on the principles of intimacy and mercy. Their purpose is relational and redemptive. There are many courts and councils in heaven. This chapter focuses on the court of accusation.

Discernment is necessary in all spiritual matters, and the courts of heaven are no exception. Some are drawn to heavenly courts without considering whether they are in submission to God. Others avoid the subject entirely out of skepticism or fear of being deceived. Both caution and courage are needed. God invites us to walk in greater authority, but authority must be used with wisdom, and in a committed relationship with Him.

Most encounters in the courts of heaven are prompted by the Holy Spirit. During prayer or worship, you may develop an awareness of God's justice or sense an accusation. You might have an impression, such as a courtroom, or see images like robes or scrolls. These experiences should be prayerfully considered. Courtroom experiences are different from other spiritual encounters. You may feel a sense of condemnation that does not come from your usual thoughts, which can be the Holy Spirit revealing an accusation from the enemy. You might see yourself before a Judge, hear arguments, or see scrolls.

In the court of accusation, God is the Judge, Jesus is our Advocate, and demons are our accusers. Generally, a demon will bring an accusation against you. In the first chapter of the book of Job, we read how Satan accused Job.

> *Then the Lord said to Satan, "Have you considered My servant Job, that there is none like him on the earth, a blameless and upright man, one who fears God and shuns evil?"*
>
> *So Satan answered the Lord and said, "Does Job fear God for nothing? Have You not made a hedge around him, around his household, and around all that he has on every side? You have blessed the work of his hands, and his possessions have increased in the land. But now, stretch out Your hand and touch all that he has, and he will surely curse You to Your face!"*
> JOB 1:8-11

Whether or not the charge brought against you is true is irrelevant. Avoid the temptation to defend yourself. The court of accusation is not about finding the truth of a matter. It is solely for the purpose of exonerating you. Once the accusation is heard, you simply plead guilty and remind the Judge that the blood of the Lamb takes away your guilt.

My own introduction to the court of heaven was unplanned and, at first, uncertain. I had been ill for four days with one of the worst viral infections I'd ever had. My wife and I had prayed. Friends were interceding, but nothing changed. On the fourth night, as I was settling in to sleep and my eyes were closed, I saw in my mind's eye what looked like a bookcase lined with law books. It was an ordinary image, not dramatic in any way. A few golden fixtures were visible nearby. The more I looked, the more the scene reminded me of my grandfather's house—he was an attorney, and his home was full of law books.

I wasn't certain what I was seeing. It could have been my imagination. But I chose to treat the image as an invitation rather than ignore it. If this were the court of heaven, then a judge must be present, I thought, even though I couldn't see one. So, I spoke aloud to a judge I couldn't see, presented my case as best I could, and pleaded the blood of Jesus. There was no response. No voice from heaven. I went to sleep not knowing whether anything had happened.

The next morning, the fever was gone.

I don't tell that story to give you a formula. What struck me most about the experience was how ordinary it felt. Just a hint of a courtroom scene, a decision to trust that it was from God, a few spoken words, and then sleep. The court of heaven is not primarily a place of spectacle. It is where the mercy of God meets the legal demands the enemy has assembled against us, and where the blood of Jesus answers every charge.

When the Judge issues a verdict in the courts of heaven, you may notice a change—a sense of peace replacing anxiety, relief from pressure, physical healing, or progress where there was delay. If you are unsure about what you experienced, write it down and pray about it.

Encounters in the courts of heaven allow us to experience God's mercy and live in freedom. If you seek courtroom experiences without first building a close relationship with God, you will miss their purpose. Stay grounded in God's love. Walk in humility. Learn from His Word. He may reveal aspects of His nature you've never seen.

CHAPTER THIRTY-NINE

Prophetic Acts

THERE ARE TIMES WHEN THE most devastating strike against the kingdom of darkness is a single, Spirit-directed act of obedience—a gesture that speaks, not to human ears, but to the unseen realm. Prophetic acts are bridges between heaven's intent and earth's terrain—physical expressions that manifest heaven's agenda and dismantle demonic resistance at its roots. They are not the products of human imagination or superstition. They are God-breathed assignments that carry the weight of His authority. In their obedience, they alter atmospheres, release miracles, sever unholy agreements, and announce verdicts issued in heaven.

A prophetic act is a Spirit-led movement in the natural world that brings about change in the spiritual realm. Scripture offers many examples: the prophet Elisha instructing a king to strike the ground with arrows, a silent march around the walls of Jericho, the tearing of a garment to signify a kingdom divided, oil poured over a young shepherd's head to crown him king, a basin of water, and the washing of feet to model the humility of the kingdom. Sometimes it was the writing of a covenant and its sealing beneath the soil, the breaking and burning of idols, or the planting of memorial stones to mark territory for God. Each of these moments carried power not because of the object or motion itself, but because the act was born in the mind of God and obeyed by a servant aligned with His heart. If God commands it, it carries weight in the courtroom above and force in the battlefield below.

The effectiveness of these actions depends on whether they are done at God's direction, in His timing, and with His authority. Sometimes, prayer or speaking God's word does not bring breakthrough because He wants a specific action to be taken. In these cases, the spoken word needs to be put into practice. This might involve walking around a property and praying, anointing the ground with oil, or sharing communion to dedicate a place to God. It could also mean destroying objects connected to past sin, removing altars, or burning documents—a sign that lies that have enslaved people are being rejected. In times of change, a prophetic act might represent a new identity or a calling, as when David removed Saul's armor. When there are ungodly agreements, a prophetic act can break them, such as tearing up a document or anointing a doorway to show that the agreement is finished. During healing ministry, when a spear or some other weapon is revealed, removing it from the afflicted person by a prophetic act can bring healing.

Just as certain actions have clear meaning in military situations, prophetic acts communicate specific messages in the spiritual realm. For example, raising a white flag means surrender, and planting a flag shows ownership. In the same way, a prophetic act signals to spiritual forces that something has changed. It shows that a place, a person, or a season is now under God's authority.

Not every symbolic action has spiritual power. Only those initiated by the Holy Spirit carry God's authority. It is important to approach these acts seriously, recognizing that some may provoke spiritual opposition.

Most prophetic acts are less dramatic than the ones found in scripture. They don't typically involve armies or city walls. More often, they are quiet, specific, and slightly awkward to explain to anyone watching. That's fine. The act doesn't need to make sense to observers. It needs to make sense to God.

History is rich with stories of such obedience. A missionary team once walked the perimeter of a war-torn village, anointing the soil with oil while singing worship into the night. Days later, enemy soldiers withdrew without explanation, and locals spoke of seeing figures of fire patrolling the ridges. A woman, weary from years of torment, burned her divorce papers during a worship service, declaring the restoration of her heart; that very night, her dreams shifted, and the shadows fled. On a university campus, young believers surrounded a prayer room with salt after repeated occult rituals had been performed nearby, and within the week, the activity ceased.

The orders stand: "Take possession of the land. I have given it into your hands." When the Spirit shows you what to do, take action. Heaven responds when we obey.

CHAPTER FORTY

Fasting

SOME SPIRITUAL BATTLES ARE NOT resolved by prayer alone. In certain situations, victory requires us to set aside physical comfort so that our spirit can become more sensitive to God. Fasting is not about enduring hunger for its own sake. It is a way to sharpen our spirit-man and overcome resistance that does not respond to ordinary means. Jesus referred to this when He said, "This kind does not go out except by prayer and fasting." There are times when demonic opposition is so entrenched that fasting is necessary to break through. Fasting is not a way to persuade God to act, nor is it a method of earning His favor. Instead, fasting helps us remove distractions and become more sensitive to God's voice. When we fast, our spiritual senses become clearer, and our prayers are more focused. Patterns of opposition are exposed, and we may receive revelation more easily because our minds are less cluttered by daily concerns. The presence of God becomes more noticeable as we set aside other influences.

Throughout scripture, we see that fasting often comes before major spiritual engagement. Jesus fasted for forty days before beginning His ministry. Moses received the Ten Commandments after fasting on the mountain. Esther and her people fasted before she approached the king. Daniel fasted and received revelation from angels. The early church fasted before sending out apostles. In each of these examples, fasting prepared people to receive guidance, revelation, and strength for what was ahead.

Fasting removes the enemy's influence in areas where we are weak or distracted. By choosing to fast, we deny the enemy access through our appetites or comforts. Fasting helps us align our will with God's, and it breaks strongholds rooted in our natural desires. It is a practical way to give our spirit-man greater control, leading to greater submission to God.

Fasting isn't needed when dealing with everyday struggles. But a stronger spirit-man is required for higher-level warfare, such as breaking generational bondage or confronting territorial spirits. Before God entrusts us with greater responsibility, fasting helps us prepare by refining our motives and making us more sensitive to His direction. God does not withhold authority, but He wants us to be ready to handle it wisely.

There are different ways to fast. Some people abstain from all food for a period of time, while others follow a partial fast like Daniel, avoiding certain foods. Some may skip meals to spend more time in prayer, or choose to fast from distractions such as media or social activities. The effectiveness of fasting is not in the specific method, but in our willingness to obey God and set ourselves apart for Him. Fasting removes lesser things to make room for what God wants to do.

Fasting demonstrates a spiritual principle: when we set aside our natural strength, God's power is made stronger in us. Paul wrote, "When I am weak, then I am strong." As we rely less on ourselves and more on God, our spiritual sensitivity and dependence on Him increase.

Consider Esther. She was not a professional intercessor. She was a young woman in an impossible position, facing a threat she had not chosen and could not outmaneuver by natural means. The demonic spirit animating Haman's plot was not only antisemitic—it was territorial, political, and murderous. It had already shaped policy and bent the ear of the king. Esther's weapon was not her beauty or her charm, but her consecration. She called her people to three days without food or water, aligning them with heaven's agenda before she dared to stand before the earthly throne. The real battle was won in the spiritual realm; her audience with the king was simply the final movement of a victory that had already been secured.

When fasting is woven together with worship, prophetic declaration, intercession, and the counsel of the wise, it strengthens every weapon in the arsenal. The atmosphere shifts under worship, legal authority is established through decrees, heavenly verdicts are released in the courts of heaven, and prophetic acts seal what has been won. Fasting does not replace these weapons; it makes them burn hotter, fly truer, and strike deeper.

We do not fast to earn God's love or acceptance—those are already settled. We do it to draw closer to Him and align ourselves with His purposes. During a fast, be mindful of your thoughts and emotions, as you may be more sensitive than usual. Always let the Holy Spirit guide you on when and how to fast.

God does not require our hunger, but He honors it. Jesus said, "Blessed are those who hunger and thirst for righteousness, for they shall be filled." When we fast in faith, heaven draws near. There are battles that simply will not be won any other way. When you sense that kind of resistance, fasting may be the next step.

CHAPTER FORTY-ONE

Unanswered Prayer

SPIRITUAL WARFARE IS, AT BOTTOM, the willful engagement in conflict. When you step into the arena, you are not stepping into a guaranteed outcome. This chapter discusses situations when the outcome is uncertain. God promises the corporate victory of His people—that is settled, and nothing will reverse it. But individual battles are another matter. The enemy has a vote, and not every skirmish will go your way. If you enter battle expecting otherwise, the first serious loss will knock you flat, and you may not get back up.

I prayed for five hundred people before I witnessed my first miracle. Five hundred. With each failure, I felt like quitting. The only thing that kept me going was that God would give me a dream in which the person I had prayed for was healed. I couldn't see it in the natural. But in the spirit, He showed me that the prayers were doing something, even when I couldn't measure it. So, I kept going.

I have lost two brothers to cancer despite my best efforts. I prayed, and I believed. I did what I was trained to do. And they are gone. There is no theological framework that takes away the pain, and I won't offer you one. When someone you love dies despite your prayers, take time to mourn the loss. When a friend you trusted turns against you, there is nothing wrong with crying your eyes out. Pain is not a sign of weakness. It is the natural response of a human being to loss. The question is not whether you allow yourself to feel it. You should. The question is whether you get stuck there.

There are seasons when I look at the direction the world is heading and wonder what the use is in praying for peace. That is my confession, and I suspect I am not alone. Discouragement is not sin. It is the cost of caring about things that don't go the way we expect. The danger is when discouragement calcifies into the conviction that nothing will ever change, because at that point you have stopped being a warrior and you've become a casualty.

The enemy would love for your losses to become your theology. He wants you to take your worst days as evidence about the nature of God, the reliability of prayer, and the value of persisting. Satan is not interested in a fair reading of your history with God. He will magnify every failure and minimize every breakthrough, because a discouraged intercessor will put down their weapons and walk off the battlefield.

This is why I do not let my losses have the last word. When I'm tempted to give up, I go back over what God has already done. I recall specific miracles—faces, names, the moment something shifted. I remember the five hundred, and I remember that I eventually saw the first one healed, and then another, and then more than I can count. That is the history that matters. It is evidence of God's goodness. And when the present circumstances loom dark, evidence is what you need.

Allow God to heal your wounded soul. The emotional toll of sustained intercession, of praying hard for someone and losing them anyway, of pouring yourself out for a situation that seems unchanged—that toll requires attention. Unprocessed grief will eventually shut down your capacity to pray with faith. Bring it to God honestly. Let Him meet you in it. That is how a warrior maintains readiness for the next engagement.

Set your mind to the task of advancing God's kingdom, knowing that loss is unavoidable but that victory is never far behind it. The two brothers I lost, I will see again. The five hundred who didn't receive their healing when I prayed—some of them may have been healed later, by someone else, in ways I was never told about. My prayers may have done more than I know. Yours will too.

The outcome of any individual battle is uncertain. The outcome of the war is not. Keep praying. Keep showing up. When you lose, take time to mourn or heal, and then get back in the fight. The next miracle is closer than you think.

CHAPTER FORTY-TWO

The Process of Breakthrough

BREAKTHROUGH.

The moment of sudden victory. And a word that has become a cliché. It is hard to find a prophetic word these days that does not promise breakthrough. But after hearing the word for years, many have quietly given up on it. They've been disappointed too often and don't want their hopes dashed again.

I wonder if the disappointment comes from not understanding what breakthrough really is.

I received a prayer request from a woman who wanted a blessing for her niece—that she would never suffer hardship, never be attacked, and always be protected from harm. I understood her heartfelt request. I have prayed for my own children's safety and protection more times than I can count. But I've come to realize that safety and protection do not always accomplish God's purposes.

It would have been easier for Jesus to avoid the temptation in the wilderness. And the betrayal of Judas. And the scourging. And the cross. But all of those painful, humiliating things were necessary. They were part of the process of learning obedience and being conformed to the will of the Father. After He had endured it, He stepped out of the tomb, more alive than He had ever been.

The breakthrough had arrived.

A bystander who knew nothing about the Lord and His suffering might have looked at the resurrection and assumed it was an event disconnected from any process. A random miracle. But we know better. Without the suffering that preceded it, the breakthrough would never have happened.

How often do we look at a person who achieved a great victory and write it off as divine favor or luck, never considering what it cost them? Many times, what appears to be a sudden breakthrough is the final stage of a long, difficult process. The emergence from a lonely walk through the valley of the shadow of death, while no one was watching.

Not everything is a process, but many things are. When we are sick, it is often because we have ignored the disciplines that would have kept us healthy. We could give up the potato chips and start exercising. But who wants all of that? We want the sickness gone, but we don't want change, especially if it means sacrifice. Change is a hassle. We want the peace, without the process.

God is more interested in our growth than our comfort. We want a life free of difficulty. He wants transformation. The difficulties we endure are intended to produce Christlike character. I would note an exception here: sickness and injury seem to lack that redemptive purpose. Jesus did not use illness to change people. He healed them. If sickness were meant to transform us, Jesus did more harm than good by removing it. But for the difficulties that are part of the transformation process such as a circumstance designed to strip away pride; a season in the wilderness where identity is rebuilt; a period of waiting that teaches perseverance—the breakthrough follows. Not as a sudden event, but as the natural outcome of a completed process.

If you are waiting for breakthrough and it has not come, it may be worth asking what process God may be inviting you into. The process will not be comfortable. But if you avoid it, the growth will not happen. And if the growth does not happen, the breakthrough cannot either. When you submit to the process, when it has done its work, you will step out of the tomb. More alive than you have ever been.

CHAPTER FORTY-THREE

Stand Your Ground

IN THE NATURAL, STANDING YOUR ground can appear almost passive—as if nothing is happening. To those watching from the outside, it may seem as though you are simply holding a position, waiting for something to change. But in the spirit, your resolute stand sends a different signal through the ranks of darkness. Scripture tells us in Ephesians 6:13, "having done all, to stand." This is not a call to idle waiting. Standing is an act of defiance—violent resistance against darkness in its purest form. It is the image of a soldier braced on the battlefield, refusing to yield even an inch of territory. Every second you remain firm, you reinforce what has been taken back from the enemy, and you bar the gates against his return.

The writer of Hebrews reminds us that we are surrounded by a great cloud of witnesses, and your perseverance echoes through that assembly. Demons notice when you do not flinch. They are meticulous observers, always gauging whether your resolve will crack. When it does not, the foundations of their influence begin to fracture. What was once a fortified wall of opposition starts to crumble, stone by stone.

Standing is more than keeping your position—it is how strong roots are established. Like a tree that faces the test of wind and storm, you develop a deep root system only when you refuse to move. These roots prepare you for lasting fruitfulness. The enemy would love for you to believe that your waiting is wasted, that stillness is stagnation, that nothing is shifting. But in reality, a foundation is being laid beneath your feet—one that will outlast the storm. The psalmist describes the righteous as a tree planted by streams of water, whose leaves do not wither. That image is not one of fragility, but of strength and endurance.

There is a strategy hidden in stillness. In 2 Chronicles 20, we read how King Jehoshaphat faced overwhelming odds and was told by the Lord, "You will not need to fight in this battle. Stand still and see the salvation of the Lord." Standing in obedience—when every impulse in you screams retreat, retaliation, or compromise—is warfare of the highest order. It is the deliberate refusal to fight in the strength of the flesh, and the conscious choice to rest in God's promise. Stillness does not mean nothing is happening; it means you have shifted the weight of the fight from your own shoulders to the hands of the One who cannot fail.

Every battle reaches a turning point—a moment when the advantage begins to tip in your favor. In the natural, it may appear small, almost inconsequential. In the spirit, it blazes like a signal fire. Elijah's servant saw a cloud no bigger than a man's hand rising over the sea, and it heralded the end of a long drought. Spiritually, such moments may take the form of a sudden lightness in your soul, a dream or vision that changes your perspective, an unexpected peace that silences inner turmoil, or a shift in relationships and circumstances that clears the way forward. Even the return of clarity and hope can be a sign that the tide is turning. Recognizing these markers helps you lean in with renewed strength rather than stepping back too soon.

When the tide begins to shift, reinforcements are often dispatched. The book of Daniel pulls back the curtain on such moments, revealing that Michael the archangel was sent to break through entrenched demonic resistance. The answer to Daniel's prayers had already been released, but persistence was required to bring it into the earth realm. When heaven moves on your behalf, you may sense a fresh surge of strength, clarity in direction, or see tangible fruit emerge in ground that was barren.

Sometimes the change manifests as confusion in the enemy's camp. Scripture speaks of the wicked being confounded and put to shame when they set themselves against the people of God. Demonic operations that once seemed well-coordinated begin to unravel. The enemy's lines of communication falter, his attacks lose their rhythm, and his agents withdraw or fall silent. You may even hear unexpected admissions from unlikely sources—proof that the grip of darkness is weakening.

When you discern that the enemy is in retreat, it is not the time to relax. It's time to move from defense to offense. David, when faced with the Amalekites who had raided his camp, sought the Lord before taking action. Once he received the command to pursue, he went forward and recovered all that had been stolen. In the same way, when the Spirit confirms that the tide has turned, you must ask, "Where and how do I press forward now?" This is the hour to reclaim what was lost, to occupy the ground that has been cleared, and to push the line of battle deeper into enemy territory.

To stand your ground in the spirit is to hold the line until heaven signals the advance. It is a stance of fierce loyalty to the victory Christ has won, an unyielding commitment to hold the territory He has entrusted to you, and a readiness to move at His word. The unseen ripple of your stand reverberates through heaven's courtrooms and the enemy's shattered lines alike, testifying that you will not be moved.

CHAPTER FORTY-FOUR

Go

You picked up this book because you sensed something of importance was at stake. Some of you are new to the subject and are looking for a place to start. Others are seasoned warriors who have been in the fight for decades, have won some victories, but still experience defeat, and you don't know why. Something brought you here. I'd like to believe it wasn't coincidence.

If you are just beginning, let me say this plainly: you are better equipped than you realize. You have the name of Jesus, the authority He purchased for you at the cross, the Holy Spirit living inside you, and the full arsenal described in these pages. You don't need more training before you start. You need to start, and the training will come through the doing. Take one step. Pray for one person. Command a demon to leave. Intercede for one situation you care about. See what happens. Then do it again.

If you have been at this for years and are tired—I hear you. I've read your emails. I understand the exhaustion that comes from a committed lifestyle of warfare. You've put it all on the line and haven't seen the results you'd hoped for. You've prayed at bedsides and stood in the gap, and persisted long after everyone else went home. That weariness is evidence of faithfulness—despite the results. The Commander knows what you're doing. Your effort is not wasted.

To both of you, I want to say the same thing: the war is difficult, but the One who sent you into it knows you are able to complete your assignments, with His help. He did not commission you and then abandon you to figure it out alone. He is present in the battle, He is ahead of the battle, and He is waiting for you at the end of it. The outcome of the war is not in question. What is still being written is your part in it—the ground you will take, the people whose lives will be changed because you showed up, the legacy you will leave for those who come after you.

You are not a bystander or an observer. You have been drafted, equipped, and sent. The territory is waiting. The assignments are ready.

Now go.

ABOUT THE AUTHOR

Praying Medic is a former atheist who has worked as a paramedic for decades. After having a dramatic encounter in which God told him He would use him to heal the sick, he began praying with his patients and with strangers, and has seen thousands of them healed. He began writing about his life as a medic in 2009, published his first book in 2013, and has since written over twenty books, spanning both fiction and non-fiction, on topics such as faith, spirituality, preparedness, and off-grid communication. His books have inspired thousands of readers to seek God for themselves. Known to friends as Dave, he's also a public speaker, teacher, and podcaster. He lives in sunny Arizona with his wife, Denise, a painter and graphic designer.

For all titles visit: PrayingMedic.com

The Red Sky Trilogy

Science Fiction

- Opturius: Beneath a Crimson Sky

Beneath a crimson sky on a distant world, a broken man dares to climb toward the unknown...

After a tragic accident leaves Adam Walker guilt-ridden and adrift, he wants nothing more than to disappear. But life has other plans. Abducted by an interstellar team and taken to the planet Opturius, Adam is asked to do the one thing he no longer believes he can.

For fans of **C.S. Lewis**, **Ursula K. Le Guin**, and **Richard Powers**, *Opturius* is a lyrical, soul-stirring journey across an alien world—where a lone climber meets the divine.

Blending spiritual depth, poetic prose, and cosmic mystery, this is science fiction for seekers—for those who believe stories should move your heart and mind.

The Kingdom of God Made Simple

- Divine Healing Made Simple
- Seeing in the Spirit Made Simple
- Hearing God's Voice Made Simple
- Traveling in the Spirit Made Simple
- Dream Interpretation Made Simple
- Power and Authority Made Simple
- Emotional Healing Made Simple
- Wisdom for Mariage Made Simple
- Freedom from Evil Spirits Made Simple

The Courts of Heaven

- Defeating Your Adversary in the Court of Heaven
- Operating in the Court of Angels

My Craziest Adventures with God

- My Craziest Adventures with God - Vol. 1
- My Craziest Adventures with God - Vol. 2

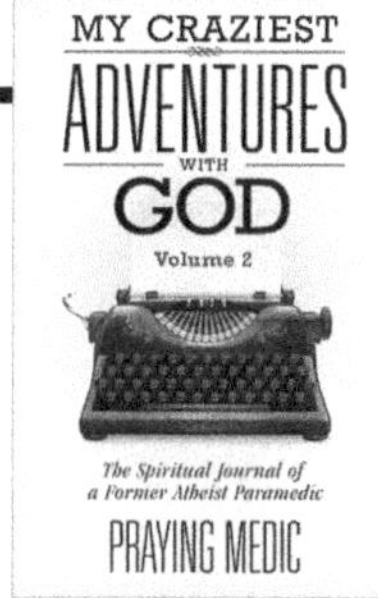

The Gates of Shiloh
(novel series)

- The Gates of Shiloh
- Charity's Garden

And more...

- Emotional Healing in 3 Easy Steps
- God Speaks: Perspectives on Hearing God's Voice

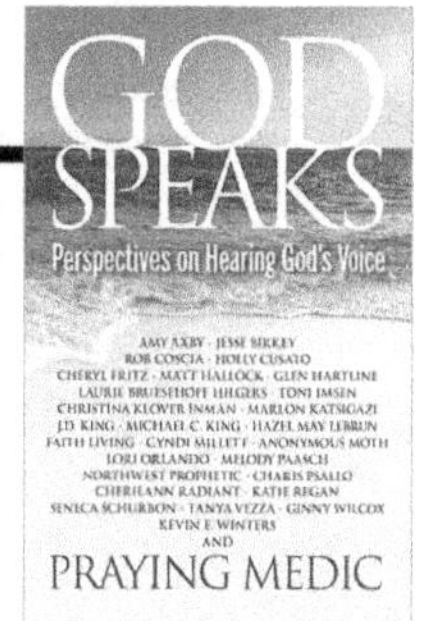

www.ingramcontent.com/pod-product-compliance
Lightning Source LLC
Chambersburg PA
CBHW051515030726
47592CB00006B/2271